When Sinners Say

When Sinners Say

"I Do"

Discovering the Power of the Gospel For Marriage

DAVE HARVEY

Shepherd Press
Wapwallopen, Pennsylvania

When Sinners Say "I Do"
©2007 by Dave Harvey
ISBN 978-0-9767582-6-6

All Scripture quotations, unless otherwise indicated, are from: The Holy Bible, English Standard Version. Copyright © 2000; 2001 by Crossway Bibles, a division of Good News Publishers. Used by Permission. All rights reserved.

Italics or bold text within Scripture quotations indicate emphasis added.

Page design and typesetting by Lakeside Design Plus
Cover design by Tobias' Outerwear for Books
Cover photo by David Sacks www.davidsacks.com

Printed in the United States of America

To Kimm,

For converting all my sounds of woe into
"hey nonny, nonny"

Twenty-five years later,
I still can't believe you said, "I do!"

Contents

Acknowledgments

For some gifted souls, writing is a solitary exercise that bubbles forth in seclusion. I marvel at that, because I'm the opposite. John Piper once wrote, "Perseverance in faith is a community project."[1] For me, so is writing.

Let me introduce you to the community of people without whom there simply would be no book. The first round of thanks goes to the immediate neighborhood—those who accepted the editorial mission to make my writing far better than it is. For over two decades, Andy Farmer has proven to be not only a trusted friend, but also a man who takes what I say and helps make it cipherable. Kevin Meath, editor-extraordinaire for Sovereign Grace Ministries at the time of writing, pushed aside a backlog of projects to serve this project. His editing resulted in a serious upgrade. Erin Sutherland, my exceptional secretary, went far beyond the call of duty by loaning her considerable talents to almost every feature of this project. To this neighborhood of colleagues, a simple thanks seems hopelessly insufficient.

Among those joining the community from a distance was C.J. Mahaney, who demonstrated his renowned kindness by advising me on the entire project. Rob Flood's keen editorial eye, sharpened in his service to Family Life Ministries, undeniably enhanced the project. Trish Donohue was also gracious to set aside the delights of domesticity long enough to help in the development of one of the chapters.

If you like the cover as much as I do, give it up for David Sacks, who sees God's activity through a camera lens and cleared a busy schedule to serve. The pastoral team of Covenant Fellowship Church deserves special thanks, not simply for restructuring things to free me up, but for allowing me the indescribable honor of leading them for the past seventeen years. And finally, my family—Kimm, Tyler, Alyce, Asa and Shelby—without your love and support, this book would be a waste of words.

That's the community who helped me. Now I know it is customary to clear these folks of responsibility for deficiencies in the book, but it seems like an unconventional book may warrant a different approach. So if you don't like the book, blame them.

Foreword

They had come to me for counseling. Now Jeff and Ellie sat across from me on opposite ends of the couch. The air was heavy with tension. They had been married for fifteen years, and had reached a point where they could barely say a civil word to one another. Almost everything they said was an accusation, their words spit out with extreme anger. My heart was sad. I knew there was a time when they had adored one another. I knew that they had once hung onto each other's words and loved each other's company. Though they had once anticipated their marriage with excitement and hope, it was now a place of anger ("I can't believe he/she did this to me!") and regret ("I wish I had never been married!").

Dave Harvey knows exactly what is wrong with this couple. He knows what has brought them from adoration to acrimony and he knows how to get them to where God designed their marriage to be. That is what I think is so practically helpful about the book that you are about to read. It is written by a man who understands. It is not because he is a pastor (although that surely helps), or a good theologian (although this book is rich with theology), or that he understands the destruction and restoration of a marriage. No—he understands what is wrong with the marriages of the Jeffs and Ellies of the world because he has been willing to look at himself in the mirror of the Word of God and admit to what he has seen there. It has been said that the best pastor is always the one who is willing to sit under his own teaching.

This book grasps the core drama of every married couple. This drama is no respecter of race, ethnic origin, location, or period of history. It is the one thing that explains the doom and hope of every human relationship. It is the theme that is on every page of this book in some way. What is this drama? It is the drama of sin and grace.

What do all of us do in our marriages in some way? We all tend to deny our sin (while pointing out the sin of the other). By denying our sin, we devalue grace. What is important about this book is that at the level of the hallways and family rooms of everyday life, it is very honest about sin and very hopeful about the amazing resources of God's grace in Jesus Christ.

I can't help but wish that Jeff and Ellie had been able to read this book. I can't help but wish I had been able to read it years ago as well, because again and again I saw myself in it.

This book reminded me once again of some very important things. It reminded me that I am my biggest marital problem (hard to accept, but biblically true). It reminded me, in ways that are very practical, that Jesus is the only solution. It encouraged me to remember that grace makes new beginnings possible. And it challenged me to live like I really believe I can be a tool of God's grace in Luella's life.

It doesn't matter whether you are looking forward to your marriage or have been married for many years. There is one thing I know for sure—your relationship isn't perfect. And because it isn't, as a couple you need to look into the mirror of God's Word once again. This book will help you to do just that.

Paul David Tripp
April 13, 2007

Preface

You might be curious about a guy who would write a book called *When Sinners Say "I Do."* My name is Dave and . . . well . . . I'm a sinner. Saying "I do" twenty-five years ago to my beautiful wife not only didn't solve that problem, it magnified it times ten. Engaged people can sometimes wonder whether "I do" holds a magical power that charms us into selfless and instinctively caring people. It doesn't. Would I have said, "I do" if I knew what "I do" really meant? Without a doubt. Would the grin in my wedding pictures have been less self-confident and more, how shall I say it, *desperate*? Most assuredly!

What do I mean when I say I'm a sinner? Picture in your mind a guy in sackcloth and ashes, prostrate on the ground, throwing dust on his head in shame.

No, scratch that. Picture this instead.

I used to have a failsafe system for vacuuming my car. Give me fifty cents and four minutes, and you could do surgery on my carpets. The key is mat placement, nimble feet, and doors ajar. Once the machine sprang to life, I would work like a human black hole, sucking everything into the vacuum that wasn't bolted down. Sure there was a cost—I lost important papers, checks and even a pet or two—but there are always casualties in the maintenance of an orderly system. It was my way. The only way.

Have you ever been so devoted to your way that it makes you, well . . . stupid?

One day at the car wash, I deposited my two coins and spun quickly to work only to crack my knee on the open door. The blunt force trauma to my knee was so sharp that both of my legs buckled. As I lay moaning, the faint hum of the vacuum cleaner pierced my consciousness reminding me that precious seconds were slipping away. I knew that the "Four-Minute-Autosweeping-System" by Dave could be compromised. Dizzy from pain and clutching my throbbing knee, I stumbled to my feet and threw myself into the car. They still talk about that spectacle at the car wash. Let it be known for the record, though, that I did successfully sweep the entire car in the requisite four minutes. Obviously, I have a pretty ridiculous drive to compete.

Maybe you think a guy who has pastored couples for over twenty-one years should be above that kind of behavior. Read on—it's worse than you think.

I have control issues. Add to that, I love to be right. That means I tend to see other peoples' opinions as inferior. I hate being wrong. Also, what people think about me sometimes determines what I do. I worry about problems I can't even solve. You'll find out a lot more about my particular package of mixed-up motivations throughout this book. But I can vouch that the more you get to know me, the more you'll admire my wife.

I found a passage from the Bible that describes the biggest problem for me and the biggest challenge in my marriage. "For the desires of the flesh are against the Spirit, and the desires of the Spirit are against the flesh, for these are opposed to each other, to keep you from doing the things you want to do" (Galatians 5:17).

14

What I love about this passage is not just that it describes my life so well; it's that it was written by somebody who you assume would have solved the sin problems of life. Isn't Paul the one who wrote, "I can do all things through him who strengthens me" (Philippians 4:13). True, but he's also the guy who confessed, "Wretched man that I am! Who will deliver me from this body of death?" (Romans 7:24).

The Apostle Paul was wretched? How does that work? Man, he must have been really bad. But what if I told you that a great marriage—a God-glorifying, soul-inspiring, life-enduring union—springs from the conviction that we are sinners just like Paul. Would that intrigue you enough to go to the next chapter? That's where we are headed, if you have the courage to come. Curious?

Let me help you with something that has helped me. To say "I am a sinner" is to stare boldly at a fundamental reality that many people don't even want to glance at. But when we acknowledge that painful reality in our lives, several great things become clear. We find ourselves in good company—the heroes of our faith, from Old Testament times to the present, who experienced the battle with sin on the front lines. We also acknowledge what everybody around us already knows— particularly our spouses. But, by far the greatest benefit of acknowledging our sinfulness is that it makes Christ and his work precious to us. Like Jesus said, "Those who are well have no need of a physician, but those who are sick. I have not come to call the righteous but sinners to repentance" (Luke 5:31–32). Only sinners need a Savior.

If you are married, or soon to be married, you are discovering that your marriage is not a romance novel. Marriage is the union of two people who arrive toting the luggage of life. And that luggage always contains sin. Often it gets opened right there on the honeymoon, sometimes it waits for the week after. But the suitcases are always there, sometimes tripping their owners, sometimes popping open unexpectedly and disgorging

15

forgotten contents. We must not ignore our sin, because it is the very context where the gospel shines brightest.

Which leads me to the point of this book. *When Sinners Say "I Do"* is not a depressing thought. It recognizes that to get to the heart of marriage, we must deal with the heart of sin. A great pastor once said, "Till sin be bitter, Christ will not be sweet."[1] He was getting at a profound truth of the gospel. Until we understand the problem, we will not be able to delight in the solution. Grace is truly amazing because of what we were saved from.

I think there's a powerful application for marriage here: *When sin becomes bitter, marriage becomes sweet.* When the sin we bring to marriage becomes real to us, then the gospel becomes vital and marriage becomes sweet.

Sound scary? Sure it does. But the gospel is good news that solves the problem of bad news. The very sin that you fear seeing is the very reason why Christ died in your place. The gospel translates our fear to worship.

> My sin, oh, the bliss of this glorious thought!
> My sin, not in part but the whole,
> Is nailed to the cross, and I bear it no more;
> Praise the Lord, praise the Lord, O my soul![2]

The next life is taken care of, so why not work on making this one even better? Your marriage can be built or rebuilt upon a solid and enduring foundation. But we must start where the gospel starts; there lies the hope for sinners who say "I do."

Chapter One

What Really Matters in Marriage

Theologians at the Altar

ulticolored beams of light sprinkled the sanctuary as the great doors swung apart. A processional hymn blended into the sweet spring air wafting through open windows. As family and friends rose to their feet, the dark wood of the pews creaked out the sound of tradition, decorum, and propriety.

Trembling imperceptibly and biting her lip for composure, the bride began her wedding march—a walk she had rehearsed in her attic for two decades. Her destination was an eager young man, a bundle of energy in a tuxedo. A smile had hijacked his face and his eyes danced with delight as he beheld his approaching bride.

The officiating minister nodded approvingly as the father of the bride made the ceremonial transfer, placing his daughter's hand in the groom's. "If there be any here," the pastor announced, "who can give a reason why this man and woman should not be joined, speak now or forever hold your peace!" All waited with polite anticipation as the clergyman paused for this obligatory nod to custom. Suddenly an old man's voice pierced the polite silence.

"How do you know?"

He stood near the back, clutching the pew in front of him, piercing eyes aflame with passion. "I mean no disrespect," he appealed, as every last face turned in his direction.

"But how do you know—I mean, really know—that this marriage is going to work?"

His tone was earnest, but not defiant. His outburst may have been startling to the congregation, but it was completely sincere.

Then, with voice and eyes lowered, his final words came slowly and deliberately.

"How . . . how can anyone know?"

Some stared at the man in wonder. Others glared their indignation. And as his unexpected question echoed softly in the rafters, it was as if time froze, while dozens of people silently formulated their answers, each hearing his own voice in his own mind.

They're in love—love can conquer anything, thought the maid of honor.

Compatibility is the key. This marriage is a lock, thought a mutual friend.

The bride and groom's former youth pastor, having known both families for years, said to himself, *It all comes down to parenting. These kids will go the distance because they've come from good families.*

Uncle Bob, the CPA, straightened his tie and chuckled to himself. *Do you have any idea what their stock portfolio is going to look like in a few years, buddy? Good financial planning eliminates the single biggest stressor to healthy marriages.*

They've read every marriage book out there—what else do they need to know? marveled the best man.

Moving into ceremony-saving mode, the pastor interjected his solution. "Dearly beloved, we are gathered here to dedicate this marriage to God. He will make it work. Let us pray . . ."

Good Question, Great Answer

Imagine if this story were true. What would you think? Who is right? All of them? None of them? What would have gone through your mind in that moment?

More importantly, how would you respond if the old man came and asked you that question about your marriage right now? Maybe for you the question isn't so much, "Will it work?" but something more like, "Can my marriage be all it should be?"

If you're reading this, the question obviously matters to you. Our goals for marriage don't stop at "will it last?" or "will it work?" What people in this most significant of relationships long for is a marriage that will thrive and grow even in hard times. So I'd like to offer an answer that might not have come to mind. It's an answer that reflects the main idea of this entire book.

First, let me say that all the answers from the astonished guests at that imaginary wedding clearly have merit: love, compatibility, strong family history, good planning, knowledge, a shared faith. Each one is a helpful or even critical component to a thriving marriage. You probably can think of other good answers too.

But there is an answer that stands behind all the others, and makes them work together in the best possible way. It's an answer so comprehensive we're going to spend the rest of this book unpacking some of its implications. It may not sound too earth-shattering at first, but based on Scripture and everything I've learned about pastoring in the last twenty-one years, I assure you that this truth can rock your world.

Here it is: *What we believe about God determines the quality of our marriage.*

Stay With Me Here

Let me take a moment to explain. Everybody views life from a perspective—what some call a worldview. Our worldview is shaped by many things: our culture, our gender, our upbringing, our present situation, etc. The most profound thing that shapes anybody's worldview is their understanding of God. What a person believes about God determines what he or she thinks about how we got here, what our ultimate meaning is, and what happens after we die. So essentially our worldview, our perspective on life, is determined by our perspective on God. And when we talk about theology, all we are talking about is what we think about God. What you truly believe about God and what it means to live for God *is* your theology. In other words, theologians aren't just really smart old guys in seminaries, or really smart dead guys in cemeteries . . . you're a theologian too! Listen to a well-known theologian of our day, R. C. Sproul:

> No Christian can avoid theology. Every Christian is a theologian. Perhaps not a theologian in the technical or professional sense, but a theologian nevertheless. The issue for Christians is not whether we are going to be theologians but whether we are going to be good theologians or bad ones.[1]

What kind of theologian are you? It's not hard to tell. Whether we realize it or not, our ideas about life, needs, marriage, romance, conflict, and everything else reveal themselves all the time in our words and deeds, inevitably reflecting our view of

God. If you listen closely, theology spills from our lips every day. See if you recognize it in this slice of conversation.

"It really frustrates me when you do that!"

"Yeah, well, whatever! That's just the way I am—it's not my fault that it pushes all the wrong buttons for you."

"You don't really care about what I need, do you?"

"What *you* need? What about what *I* need? My feelings don't seem to matter at all in this marriage."

"Why can't you trust me?"

A typical word-duel for a married couple? Perhaps. But it's far more than that. Such simple statements, which every married person might think (even if we don't always speak them), come from hearts that have adopted certain assumptions about who we are, what we need, what's really important, and how God figures into it all. In a conversation like this, theology is being backed out of the garage and taken for a spin.

That might not be obvious to you right now but I trust it will become more clear as this book progresses. A good, everyday spouse-theologian can see in this conversation that beliefs about God and self, about problems and relationships, and about right and wrong are being hotly defended and argued. It's there in the vocabulary . . . "frustrates." It's revealed in the reference points . . . "what I need." And it's displayed through the underlying assumptions . . . "just the way I am."

So make no mistake about it. How a husband and wife build their marriage day-by-day and year-by-year is fundamentally shaped by their theology. It governs how you think, what you say, and how you act. Your theology governs your entire life. And it determines how you live in your marriage.

First Things First: Lining Up the Buttons

Have you ever buttoned your shirt wrong . . . you know, so the holes and buttons don't match up and the shirt looks like it was pasted on by first-graders? (Just a hunch, but this

21

is probably a guy thing.) It happened to me recently. I got the first button in the wrong hole and kept going until I was sporting a fashion nightmare. Funny thing was, I thought I looked great—maybe I had an extra button at the bottom, but that was obviously a defect in the shirt.

Moments like this put my wife, Kimm, in an awkward position. *Should I fix him again?* she ponders, *or just allow the guys at the office to enjoy it?* This time she was merciful, and I had a properly-buttoned day.

It's amazing how distorted and disheveled one can look from not getting that first button right. Start off in the wrong place, and there's no way to correct the problem down the line. Getting the first one right is the key to getting everything else right.

Marriage is like that shirt. If you get the first things right, then the many other "buttons" of marriage—communication, conflict resolution, romance, roles—all start to line up in a way that works together.

The first button in marriage? You got it . . . theology! But what does a "rightly buttoned" theology look like? Let's look briefly at three of the most important components of a solid, biblical theology of marriage.

The Foundation of Your Marriage—The Bible

To be a good theologian and therefore a good spouse, we must study God as he really is. We must get our understanding and interpretation of God and reality from Scripture. It is in Scripture that God is revealed truly—his character, his activity, his heart, and his glorious, redemptive plan. Most profoundly, in the Bible we encounter God as he has ultimately made himself known in the person of Jesus Christ. Christ is "the truth" (John 14:6). To know him is to know the truth. Truth-based marriages are inherently centered on Christ.

We obviously live in a day when the meaning of marriage is up for grabs. Unfettered from any source of authority, marriage follows culture . . . no matter where culture goes. After a head-banging night of partying, one pop idol got married, then had the marriage annulled in the morning. To her, marriage may have simply seemed like a fun thing to do for a few hours, not too different from an afternoon at the mall or a visit to Starbucks. Just a spontaneous indulgence. No harm done.

This is why the Bible is so important. As God's Word, it fills marriage with eternal and glorious significance. It also speaks as an authority on what a marriage is meant to be. It is both the evaluative standard for marriage and the key to joy in marriage. It's a wonderful, freeing thing to realize that the durability and quality *of* your marriage is not ultimately based on the strength of your commitment *to* your marriage. Rather, it's based on something completely *apart from* your marriage: God's truth; truth we find plain and clear on the pages of Scripture.

I know an engineer with a job way too complicated for me to even begin to understand. Not long ago he told me about a computer program with an operating manual that required the personal explanation of its creator. Engineers from all over the world flew to this inventor for sessions on how to interpret the manual and use the program. The thinking was that he created the program, he wrote the manual, he's the authority . . . let's start there! Makes sense to me.

This makes sense in marriage too. God created the marriage "program," wrote the "operating manual," and is faithful to explain it. He is the one and only reliable and trustworthy authority on the subject of marriage. As its "inventor" (see the first two chapters of Genesis), he knows how it works and how to make it last. Lord over marriage, he has given all we need for life and godliness—and marriage—in his Word.

The Bible is the foundation for a thriving marriage.

The Fountain of Your Marriage—The Gospel

If we want to live with the Bible as the foundation for marriage, let's make sure we're clear on what it's really all about. Here's a quick overview of the Bible's perspective.

Well, let's see . . . in the first two chapters of Genesis we see that God created man and woman to live in dependence on God and for the glory of God. Yet, three chapters into the Bible, they have turned away from God to themselves—sin has entered the picture. As a direct result, they lose the extraordinarily personal relationship they had enjoyed with God–a break that will affect every person who comes after them. Many, *many* pages later, at the very end of the book of Revelation, God has completely restored that personal relationship lost by Adam and Eve and has created a new heavens and new earth for his people.

Let's see—there was a relationship broken by sin in the distant past. Then, because sin has been removed, the relationship is fully restored at some point in the future. Pretty clear pattern there. Now, what happens with the sixty-four books in between? The gospel, that's what happens. God sent his Son as the answer for the sin dilemma, not just to be an example of moral goodness or teach us the way to live, but to take the judgment for sin promised in Genesis 3, so that we might live in restored relationship with God forever.

The gospel is the heart of the Bible. Everything in Scripture is either preparation *for* the gospel, presentation *of* the gospel, or participation *in* the gospel. In the life, death, and resurrection of Christ, the gospel provides an ultimate solution for our sin—for today, for tomorrow, for the day we stand before God, and forever.

There really is no end to the glories of the gospel, which is why we will spend eternity marveling that the Holy God would choose to crush his only Son for the sake of sinful man. The gospel explains our most obvious and basic problem—sin has separated us from God and from each other. Thus we are objects of God's wrath. A Christian understands the necessity of the cross; our sin was so bad that it required blood, the blood of God, to take it away! Without the cross we are at war with God, and he is at war with us.

The gospel is therefore central to all theological truth, and is the overarching reality that makes sense of all reality. Never make the mistake of thinking that the gospel is only good for evangelism and conversion. *By* the gospel we understand that, although saved, we remain sinners. *Through* the gospel we receive power to resist sin. Accurately understanding and continually applying the gospel *is* the Christian life.

This also means that the gospel is an endless fountain of God's grace in your marriage. To become a good theologian and to be able to look forward to a lifelong, thriving marriage, you must have a clear understanding of the gospel. Without it, you *cannot* see God, yourself, or your marriage for what they truly are.

The gospel is the fountain of a thriving marriage.

The Focus of Your Marriage—the Glory of God

When we begin to orient our marriages around biblical truth, we see something amazing. Marriage was not just *invented* by God, it *belongs* to God. He has a unique claim over its design, purpose, and goals. It actually exists for him *more* than it exists for you and me and our spouses.

That's right. Marriage is not first about me or my spouse. Obviously, the man and woman are essential, but they are also secondary. God is the most important person in a marriage. Marriage is for our good, but it is first for God's glory.

That may seem odd, surprising, or difficult to accept, but it's a vital truth for every Christian married couple. A church service can inject religious formalities into a wedding, but to make God the authority for marriage is a daily reality.

In my pastoral ministry, I've seen the sad fruit of the failure to give to God what is rightly his.

- Young couples running headlong into romance, disregarding the wisdom of those closest to them, trying to use marriage as a way to legitimize uncontrolled desires. They did not see marriage as first being about God.
- Christian married couples cashing in their biblical roles and marital responsibilities in favor of "what works," even if that means settling for far less than what could be. They did not see marriage as first being about God.
- Most tragic of all, Christian families torn apart by divorce when one or both spouses simply decide that personal need is more important than what God has joined together. They did not see marriage as first being about God.

The Apostle Paul spends much of the fifth chapter of Ephesians talking to married people. Having already outlined in prior chapters what Christ has done for them as individuals, he then calls husbands and wives "to walk in a manner worthy of the calling to which you have been called" (Ephesians 4:1). Chapter 5 is filled with specific directives for building marriages that thrive. The most notable thing about Paul's approach is that *Christ is the reference point for all our actions in marriage.*

Wives are to submit to husbands "as to the Lord" (v. 22). Husbands are to love wives "as Christ loved the church and gave himself up for her" (v. 25). Husbands should nourish and cherish wives, "just as Christ does the church" (v. 29). In each case we see that while the action belongs to us, there is another and greater drama taking place through those actions.

We see that drama again in verse 32, where something glorious and mystifying is taking place. "This mystery is profound, and I am saying that it refers to Christ and the church." Commentator George Knight provides this helpful insight:

> Unbeknownst to the people of Moses' day (it was a "mystery"), marriage was *designed by God* from the beginning to be a picture or parable of the relationship between Christ and the church. Back when God was planning what marriage would be like, He planned it for this great purpose: it would give a beautiful earthly picture of the relationship that would someday come about between Christ and His church. This was not known to people for many generations, and that is why Paul can call it a "mystery." But now in the New Testament age Paul reveals this mystery, and it is amazing.
>
> This means that when Paul wanted to tell the Ephesians about marriage, he did not just hunt around for a helpful analogy and suddenly think that "Christ and the church" might be a good teaching illustration. No, it was much more fundamental than that: Paul saw that *when God designed the original marriage He already had Christ and the church in mind.* This is one of God's great purposes in marriage: to picture the relationship between Christ and His redeemed people forever![2]

I think that qualifies as profound. Marriage is set within the world—and within your home and mine—as a reminder, a living parable of Christ's relationship to the church.

The months of preparation, the Big Day, the memorable honeymoon—these are all important, but there's something more important at stake than a great wedding album. When a man and woman are joined in marriage, a new and lifelong model of the relationship between Christ and his church is launched.

How easy it is to act as if husband and wife are the only relevant parties in a marriage. But marriage is ultimately about God. Moreover, marriage is most amazing not because it brings people joy, or allows for a nurturing environment for children, or because it stabilizes society (even though it does all those things). Marriage is awesome because God designed it to display his glory.

The focus of a thriving marriage is the glory of God.

Marriage is Street-Level Theology

Okay, so we've started to build a clear, accurate, biblical theology of marriage. But if your marriage is anything like mine, you don't live out your theology in some ivory-tower world of peaceful libraries and deep thoughts. We are street theologians, trying to exercise our faith in a world where couples get angry and doors get slammed.

So with the good news of the gospel in mind—that Christ came into the world to save sinners—I have to ask the dumb question of the week . . . do you still sin? Does your spouse? Let me make it easy for you.

Guys, the radiant woman on whose finger you slipped that wedding ring? . . . *sinner*. Ladies, the man who offered you a vow of perfect faithfulness and lifelong sacrifice? . . . *sinner*. In ceremonies all over the world, every day, without exception, it is sinners who say, "I do." It is sinners who celebrate their tenth anniversary, their twenty-fifth, and their fiftieth. It is sinners who share a final kiss at a spouse's deathbed. It is a sinner who wrote this book. And it is sinners who are reading it.

The daily struggle with sin experienced by genuine Christians underscores the fact that while Christ certainly saved us, he does not transform us instantly and completely into non-sinners. That glorious process begins the moment we are converted, and continues throughout our life on earth, but it will only be finished when we leave this fallen world.

That's why here in the first chapter—and even in the title of this book!—I have tried to emphasize and personalize the reality of sin. God is changing us sinners. That process of change points toward a glorious goal—to become more like his Son, our Savior. But for us to become more like Christ, we must reckon with the fact that we are sinners; forgiven, yes, but still battling the inward drive to turn away from God to ourselves.

Without such biblical clarity, we have no context for the cross and no ongoing awareness of our need for grace and mercy. Without a robust perspective on sin, the very notion of what it means to know God is profoundly weakened. Cornelius Plantinga noted, "[T]he sober truth is that without full disclosure on sin, the gospel of grace becomes impertinent, unnecessary, and finally uninteresting."[3] Without a "full disclosure on sin," blind self-confidence will compel us to try to make our marriages work on our own strength. And whatever we try to do in our own strength does not have as its goal the glory of God and does not get its life from the fountain of the gospel.

If your honeymoon is a distant memory and your marriage has lost some of the fire and spark, and if you wonder how you have ended up calling your snookums "Mommy" or "Daddy" (and not just in front of the kids), consider this: What if you abandoned the idea that the problems and weaknesses in your marriage are caused by a lack of information, dedication, or communication? What if you saw your problems as they truly are: caused by a war within your own heart?

If you happen to be reading this book in the glow of a blissful honeymoon, now would be a good time to lean over to your sugarplumhoneykins and whisper softly, "I'm a really big sinner—and I'm yours for life."

That's how you do street theology in marriage.

Till sin be bitter, Christ will not be sweet

In this book, I want to convince you that dealing with the sin problem is key to a thriving marriage. When we apply the gospel to our sin, it gives us hope in our personal lives and in our marriages. Bad news leads to great news. It's the story of the Bible, and the story of our lives.

The great pastor I mentioned in the preface was Thomas Watson. Remember his words? "Till sin be bitter, Christ will not be sweet." He means that until we truly understand the problem, we won't savor the solution. Isn't that your testimony? Haven't you seen that the more clearly you comprehend the scope of sin's awfulness, the more quickly you flee to the Savior, now revealed anew in his glory, holiness, beauty, and power?

Looking first at our own sin as a root cause of the problems in our marriages is not easy, and it certainly doesn't "come naturally." The sin that remains in your heart and mine opposes God and his people. It obstructs our joy and our holiness. It eclipses thriving, healthy marriages which are testimonies to God's goodness and mercy.

But as we begin to build our marriages on the Word of God and on the gospel of Christ's victory over the power of sin, as we face the sad, painful, undeniable reality of our own remaining sin . . . as we see it for the bitter, hateful thing it is . . . and as we recognize sin's insidious goals at the core of every relational difficulty we encounter, something wonderful happens. We flee to the gospel as our only remedy.

Then we begin to realize there is new hope for our marriages. A lot of hope. Hope that emerges from the power of the gospel, the very power that raised Christ from the tomb. We get a glimpse of the sweet relationship our marriage can become—a living, thriving union where sins are confessed and forgiven. My friends, when sin becomes bitter, marriage becomes sweet.

Like that old man who interrupted an otherwise lovely wedding, many of us have been saddened by marriages that start sweet but don't stay that way. Every "I do" comes with a hope that devoted love will endure. But how can we be certain? How do we know that our marriages will not merely last, but thrive, becoming sweeter and more delightful with the passage of time?

What we're really in pursuit of is a marriage that thrives, that glows ever brighter, that looks and works and feels like what we had hoped for at the beginning—maybe even beyond what we had hoped. To promote enjoyable God-glorifying marriages is why I'm writing this book. I hope that's what you're looking for by reading it.

Where We Go From Here

Twenty-five years ago, in a stairwell at my college, I sang Kimm a song and then asked her to marry me. Anyone who has heard me sing would have bet against her accepting my offer. But she said, "Yes!" Little did I know of the adventure that God had in store.

We now have four kids and a cat. I don't like cats, but I'm wildly in love with Kimm, and because *she* loves cats, I manage to tolerate this one.

Our lives are complicated; "careening" is probably a better word. Our marriage is a rich, sweet chaos. But our journey is sustained, through the grace of God, by a passionate companionship that grows deeper every year. It is a mystery to me, but not to God. It was his idea to exalt his name when sinners say "I do."

Because of the grace of God, and the counsel of the men to whom I am accountable in my local church, and a lot of wonderful teaching, more often than not the buttons in our marriage are lined up reasonably well. It started years ago when we began learning a simple truth about the importance of paying close attention to God's Word. "What comes into our minds when we think about God," said A. W. Tozer, "is the most important thing about us." That's button number one in my book, and it's why I emphasize "seeing God, yourself, and your marriage for what they truly are."[4]

As you come to the end of this first chapter, perhaps you realize you have some buttons out of place. Maybe you are beginning to sense that if your experience of sin is not all that bitter, and your experience of marriage not all that sweet, maybe your theology is not all that it should be.

That's okay. Stick with me for the rest of this book and I'll do my best to pass along a lot of wonderful stuff about marriage that I've learned from Scripture and from others far wiser than I am. We will see that sin, although deceitful, is at the same time surprisingly predictable. We will probe the glorious mysteries of mercy, grace, and forgiveness, and see how these can become practical, powerful tools in the hands of a good spouse-theologian. We will examine a variety of ways we can help and serve our spouses, from the heat of confrontation to the warmth of sexual intimacy. And we will look ahead to the day when our time on earth grows short, and see what it means to honor God in marriage when our flesh grows weak.

Could it be that you and your beloved are actually sinners? Then this book is for you! And could it be that God already *knows* you are sinners, yet gives you everything you need to build a thriving marriage *anyway*? God is completely, totally, enthusiastically supportive of your every effort to build a strong, God-glorifying marriage. He wants us to delight in marriage. He wants to make it strong, make it stick, and make it sweet.

Come on, let's find out what it really means to see God, yourself, and your marriage for what they truly are. That's where it all begins.

Chapter Two

Waking Up With the Worst of Sinners

The News About Who We Really Are

Sigh . . . I'd done it again.

My wife had been running a little behind our intended schedule. Rather than waiting patiently (or maybe actually stepping in to help) I did what I do so well: I pontificated, this time speculating aloud about how many total minutes of our lives she had wasted in delays. My calculations didn't impress her, but the soul-crushing impact of my words was obvious on her face. *Very smooth, Dave, I* realized too late, *very constructive. A true word in season.*

You'd think a pastor, someone called to think and speak in thoughtful, helpful, biblical ways, would have found something better to say at that moment—or at least something a little less damaging. But despite my arrogant, sinful words, Kimm was able once again to cover them over with love and patiently help me see what was wrong with them.

While I'm immensely grateful for Kimm's gracious, forgiving spirit, still the question lingers: *Why aren't I more loving?* After all, we have been married for more than two decades. I have been in ministry most of that time, I've read lots of marriage books, conducted numerous marriage seminars, and I really think Kimm is a gift from God to me. *If I love my wife, why do I find it so easy to treat her like I don't?*

It happens with the kids also. The other day, one was acting in a way that required what my grandmother used to call "a speakin' to." Once again the Great Pontificator opened his trap. Rather than taking this opportunity to care for my child graciously, my words were harsh and critical. Different issue, different person, same problem: I treated someone I love as if I had no love at all.

Guys, you know the kind of thing I'm talking about. You've planned a romantic evening, complete with her favorite restaurant. But then she says something, or you say something, or the waiter says something, and in the space of about two minutes a whole different kind of memory is created. ("Honey, remember the night we had that really expensive conflict?")

Or how about this? Rather than watching the football game on your day off, you decide to do the repair project she's been asking you to finish. Five frustrating hours later you put the tools away, and look to your wife for some expression of appreciation for your personal sacrifice. She glances at your work and says, "I wish you would have asked me before you did it that way." Cue the pyrotechnics.

Ladies, he tells you he'll be home by 9:00 p.m. and walks in at 10:45. "Sorry, hon, the meeting ran over." No notification, no phone call, no *real* apology, and no consideration for your worry. A moment earlier you'd been imagining how you were going to manage supporting your family as a widow. Now, with visions of him sleeping in the car for a week, you're not quite sure what's about to come out of your mouth, but it probably won't be good.

Paul's Confession and Ours

It's the underside of marriage, the reality of living with someone day in and day out in a fallen world. But what does it reveal? What does it indicate when I see my rottenness? Has the enemy singled me out for exclusive attention? Maybe I'm a threat to his kingdom, like Frodo to the powers of Mordor or Luke Skywalker to the Evil Empire. That doesn't excuse the fact that I know what's right, yet often choose to do something else instead.

Well, guess what? If sin is a persistent problem for us, we're in pretty good company. As bad as we can be, the Apostle Paul seems to think he's even worse. Maybe we can learn something from him.

Paul wrote to Timothy, "The saying is trustworthy and deserving of full acceptance, that Christ Jesus came into the world to save sinners, of whom I am the foremost" (1 Timothy 1:15). Pretty stark, isn't it? Not a lot of wiggle room there. Paul leads off by calling this a "saying [that] is trustworthy and deserving of full acceptance." That's the ancient equivalent of putting the little exclamation mark on an email you send—this is of high priority!

His "saying" has two parts. "Christ Jesus came into the world to save sinners . . ." This catapults us to the heart of the glorious gospel, and prepares us for part two: ". . . of whom I am the foremost." Now what are we supposed to do with that? How can the Apostle to the Gentiles—the original theologian of the Christian faith—honestly say this? To whom is he comparing himself? And what standard is he applying?

These are important questions. We dare not dismiss Paul's statement as a passing exaggeration or an empty exercise in false humility. This is the Word of God, and a profound point is being made here.

First, it's clear that Paul is *not* trying to objectively compare himself to every other human being, because most of them he had never met! This tells us that his focus is not primarily outward. It's inward. He's also not suggesting that his moral character is bankrupt or his spiritual maturity is zero. He is simply talking about what goes on in his own heart.

He is saying, in effect, "Look, I know my sin. And what I've seen in my own heart is darker and more awful; it's more proud, selfish, and self-exalting; and it's more consistently and regularly in rebellion against God than anything I have glimpsed in the heart of anyone else. As far as I can see, the biggest sinner I know is me."

Paul was a student of his heart. He paid attention to the desires and impulses that churned within. And I don't think it's a stretch to say that he knew he was capable—given the right circumstances—of the worst of sins and the vilest of motives. Paul was a realist. He wanted to see God and himself *truly*. No hiding behind a facade of pleasantness or religiosity for him. As Henry Scougal comments on this verse, "None can think more meanly of [Paul] than he doth of himself."[1]

Now let's look at the very next verse. "But I received mercy for this reason, that in me, as the foremost, Jesus Christ might display his perfect patience as an example to those who were to believe in him for eternal life" (1 Timothy 1:16).

With the passing of each day, two things grew larger for Paul: his sinfulness in light of the holiness of God, and God's mercy in the face of his sin. Knowing both God and himself accurately was not at all discouraging or depressing. Rather, it deepened his gratitude for the vastness of God's mercy in redeeming him, and the patience of Christ in continuing to love and identify with him in his daily struggle against sin.

Paul's confession to Timothy above presents us with a stunning example of moral honesty and theological maturity: Paul's acute, even painful awareness of his own sinfulness caused him to magnify the glory of the Savior!

The Biblical Reality of Joyful Wretches

This profound awareness of innate sinfulness is not some obscure theological point or an example of religious fervor gone to seed. A great awareness of one's sinfulness often stands side by side with great joy and confidence in God. The same Paul who could call himself the foremost of sinners could exult two verses later, "To the King of ages, immortal, invisible, the only God, be honor and glory forever and ever. Amen" (1 Timothy 1:17).

It is a theme that also resonates through the Psalms. In Psalm 40 we see rejoicing in the Lord and lamentation over sin side by side.

> As for you, O Lord, you will not restrain
> your mercy from me;
> your steadfast love and your faithfulness will
> ever preserve me!
> For evils have encompassed me
> beyond number;
> my iniquities have overtaken me,
> and I cannot see;
> they are more than the hairs of my head;
> my heart fails me.

What's going on here? Is this some kind of bipolar spirituality at work? By no means! It is the joy of salvation breaking through, despite life in a fallen world and a heart still fighting against sin. It is reality as seen through biblical truth.

This reality is very different from what we're usually up to our necks in—that slick, shiny, false reality of an affluent, comfort-driven society obsessed with self-esteem. Instead, this reality sends us to the Savior, who brings God's holiness and mercy together in the cross. The great nineteenth century preacher, Charles Spurgeon, was another man who saw this reality in all its Christ-centered glory.

> Too many think lightly of sin, and therefore think lightly of the Savior. He who has stood before his God, convicted and condemned, with the rope about his neck, is the man to weep for joy when he is pardoned, to hate the evil which has been forgiven him, and to live to the honour of the Redeemer by whose blood he has been cleansed.[2]

Remember what Jesus said of the woman caught in adultery? "Therefore I tell you, her sins, which are many, are forgiven—for she loved much. But he who is forgiven little, loves little" (Luke 7:47). If like Paul (and David and Spurgeon . . .) I recognize the enormity of my sin, seeing myself as the worst of sinners, then I understand I have been forgiven *much*. That's when biblical reality begins to make sense. I start to see God as he truly is. His vastness becomes bigger than my problems. His goodness comes to me even though I'm not good. And his wisdom and power are visible in the perfect ways he works to transform me from the inside out.

So this sin—my sin and yours—is supremely ugly. It is vile. It is wicked. But at the same time it is the backdrop to a larger drama. We may be works in progress who are painfully prone to sin, yet we can be joyful works, for—thanks be to God—we have been redeemed by grace through the death and resurrection of Christ. Our Savior has come to rescue us from the penalty of sin and grant us an abundant life by his Spirit.

As two people in marriage embrace this view of reality, and live in accordance with it, their lives and marriage begin to look more and more like the picture God wants to display to a lost world. Until sin be bitter, marriage may not be sweet.

Rob, Sally, and the Rest of Us

Rob and Sally have been Christians for a long time. Like many couples, they have each adopted certain assumptions about how the other should behave, and they each feel they have certain needs that they think the other should meet. And although they attend church and live conscientious Christian lives, Rob and Sally are experiencing serious marital conflict. What they don't see is that their fights are grounded in wrong views of reality, so meaningful solutions always seem to escape them.

Here are just a couple of examples. Rob says he needs respect, but all he seems to get are Sally's critical comments each evening when he comes home from work. Sally says she needs Rob to reach out to her and provide a greater sense of security in their marriage, but all she seems to get is Rob's passivity day after day. There is really nothing wrong with these particular desires. The problems emerge when, several times a week, they rehearse each other's failures, reiterate their demands for change, and repeat (with slight variations) the kind of hurtful remarks they've been tossing back and forth for months. Curiously—and tragically—Rob and Sally both feel vindicated by many of the marriage books they've read, books which feed their sense of justice denied and seem to legitimize the needs they feel so deeply.

As a friend witnessing the gradual erosion of Rob and Sally's marriage, how would you try to help? Sure, they need a listening ear that tries to understand them both. But their greatest need is in their theology. They must recognize that some of the expectations they hold for one another—and the underlying perspectives from which these expectations emerge—are unbiblical. Certainly their accusations, harsh words, and selfishly demanding attitudes are riddled with sin. As a couple, they need help aligning themselves with Scripture—with God's view of reality.

Rob and Sally's root problem is revealed in the fact that Paul's saying in 1 Timothy 1:15 is not yet "trustworthy" to them. The sincere recognition and honest ownership of their own individual sinfulness does not have "full acceptance." Like many married believers, Rob and Sally have melted down Paul's trustworthy saying and recast it into an unbiblical mold: "Christ Jesus came into the world to . . . meet my needs, *of which I have the most!*"

In short, Rob and Sally lack understanding of how the gospel really works; they are far from alone. John MacArthur laments the widespread loss of biblical reality among believers:

> Christians are rapidly losing sight of sin as the root of all human woes. And many Christians are explicitly denying that their own sin can be the cause of their personal anguish. More and more are attempting to explain the human dilemma in wholly unbiblical terms: temperament, addiction, dysfunctional families, the child within, codependency, and a host of other irresponsible escape mechanisms promoted by secular psychology.
>
> The potential impact of such a drift is frightening. Remove the reality of sin, and you take away the possibility of repentance. Abolish the doctrine of human depravity and you void the divine plan of salvation. Erase the notion of personal guilt and you eliminate the need for a Savior.[3]

This ongoing need for the Savior is exactly what professing Christians must hang on to. The cross makes a stunning statement about husbands and wives: we are sinners and our only hope is grace. Without a clear awareness of sin, we will evaluate our conflicts outside of the biblical story—the finished work of Jesus Christ on the cross—thus eliminating any basis for true understanding, true reconciliation, or true change. Without the gospel of our crucified and risen Savior our marriages slide toward the superficial. We begin to make limp justifications for our sinful behavior, and our marriage conflicts end, at best, in uneasy, partial, negotiated settlements.

But once I find 1 Timothy 1:15–16 trustworthy—once I can embrace it with full acceptance—once I know that I am indeed the worst of sinners, then my spouse is no longer my biggest problem: *I am*. And when I find myself walking in the shoes of the worst of sinners, I will make every effort to grant my spouse the same lavish grace that God has granted me.

The Worst Thing About Sin

By this time you may be saying to yourself, *This guy thinks about sin way too much! The worst of sinners? Man, take a chill pill and unplug the moral meter. What's the big deal?*

The big deal is that my sin is not first against me or my marriage. All sin is first against God. And that changes everything.

Look at it this way. My status as "husband" says something important about me: It says I have a wife. In identifying me it points to the reality of another—my wife. It also indicates who I am *not*, for if I am a husband, I'm obviously not single.

Now recall that the Bible has a specific way of describing human beings—as sinners (Psalm 51:5, Romans 3:23; 5:12). We are all in that category together. It's hardly an exclusive club. To accept the designation of "sinner" is to acknowledge who I am *in relation to God*. It also says who I am not: I am not a neutral actor. By my very nature (which is sinful), I am an offense to God's very nature (which is perfectly holy).

So the term "sinner," when used in Scripture, clearly implies there is one (*at least* one) who is sinned against. When I speak a critical, unkind word to Kimm in front of our children, my sin is to some degree against the children. Obviously, it is to a much stronger degree against Kimm. What I need to see, however, is that this sin is most strongly, and therefore primarily, against God! And *that* is something it has in common

41

with every other sin that has ever been or ever will be committed. Every sin, however small or great its apparent impact on people, violates the purity of the perfectly just and holy God. Sin is always aimed first and foremost at God (Deuteronomy 9:16, 1 Samuel 15:24, Psalm 51:4). Jerry Bridges brings it smack into the family room when he writes,

> Sin is wrong, not because of what it does to me, or my spouse, or child, or neighbor, but because it is an act of rebellion against the infinitely holy and majestic God.[4]

Several years ago I became aware of a subtle, destructive habit. Whenever I sensed I had sinned against Kimm I would go to her, confess, and seek to resolve the situation. Looks pretty good when I put it that way, doesn't it? But I came to realize that my goal was far from noble. I wanted a quick and efficient restoration of our relationship so I could stop feeling bad and get on with "more important things." In other words, the confession was basically a tool I was employing for my own sake. No wonder, then, that I was often left with a shallow, haunting feeling that I now believe was the kind prompting of the Holy Spirit.

After a time of prayer, I recognized that God had been surprisingly forgotten in my words of apology to Kimm. I saw that I had been almost completely unconcerned with the fact that my sin had been first against God, and that I stood guilty before his infinite holiness. I had regarded my sins as errors, or at worst, as "little sins" that required little consideration of my heart. My real goal was simply a kind of marital damage control, not an honest accounting before my Heavenly Father. But by God's grace I began to see, as J. I. Packer says so well, "There can be no small sins against a great God."[5]

As biblical reality started to sink in, amazing things happened. I began to experience true sorrow for my "little sins." My awareness of God and his mercy grew. In my marriage I began to notice the very real but less obvious sins I was regularly committing against Kimm—sins we had become "comfortable with" but they, nevertheless, were slowly eroding our relationship. I began to recognize situations where I might be tempted to sin against her, and I started to learn how to battle those temptations. My confessions, as well as our conversations about the problems in our marriage, began to have a rich and satisfying depth. These conversations were not always easy, but definitely helpful to our relationship. I had come to see God, myself, and my marriage a little more clearly.

Worst of Sinners–Best of Worlds!

So here is my conclusion: I am a better husband and father, and a happier man, when I recognize myself as the worst of sinners. That status just seems more obvious to me with the passing of each week. But then again, you're the worst of sinners too. So is your spouse. At least it's not lonely here at the bottom.

Do you fear that you'll be too hard on yourself? If so, just remember that to Paul, his "worst of sinners" view was a sign of clear-eyed self-assessment and a robust awareness of the holiness of God. Remember also who we are in Christ *despite* our sin: we are treasured children of the Father, who loved us enough to send his only Son to suffer the punishment for our sins, even those sins we have yet to commit. And remember that God is at work in you, conforming you into a genuine, from the inside out, example of Christ. A sober assessment of our sinful condition doesn't hinder that work, it celebrates it!

The question that used to boggle my mind, "*If I love my wife, why do I find it so easy to treat her like I don't?*" has a universal answer. We are all the worst of sinners, so anything we do that *isn't* sin is simply the grace of God at work. In the next chapter we'll discuss how to employ that grace to fight the battle that comes from being both the worst of sinners and a child of God. But we shouldn't end this chapter without appreciating the hidden gift that comes as we see ourselves as the worst of sinners.

It is humility—a pride-crushing, vision-clearing humility. "There are two things that are suited to humble the soul of men," John Owen wrote, "a due consideration of God, and then of ourselves. Of God, in his greatness, glory, holiness, power, majesty, and authority; of ourselves, in our mean, abject, and sinful condition."[6]

The road of humility is open to all husbands and wives who are willing to give "a due consideration" to who they truly are, in and of themselves, before a holy God. I want to walk that road. I know you do too, or you wouldn't be reading this book. In these first two chapters you've confronted some uncomfortable truths. I hope you are sensing the promise that God holds out to those who acknowledge their sinfulness with humility. There's nothing quite like being a forgiven sinner, grateful to the living God for life, breath, salvation, and every other provision. It's really the only perspective from which you can begin to see God, yourself, and your marriage in true reality.

But hold on. In the next chapter we'll be taking a closer look at these things; this journey is about to get even more exciting.

Chapter Three

The Fog of War
and the Law of Sin

Preparing for the Inevitable

July 21, 1861. The first major battle of the Civil War started before dawn. The roar of artillery seemed to awaken everyone in Virginia as the Union and Confederate armies clashed among the farms by a stream called Bull Run. But a strange thing happened as the battle intensified. Hundreds of Washingtonians—Senators, Representatives, government workers and their families, all dressed in leisure apparel and carrying picnic baskets—raced to the hill near Manassas to watch the battle unfold. Armed with opera glasses to survey the fighting, they chatted amicably as men were slaughtered on the fields below. One northern sympathizer commented, "That is splendid. Oh my! Is not that first rate? I guess we will be in Richmond this time tomorrow."[1]

Spirits were high, toasts were raised. All in all, they thought it a superb way to spend a summer afternoon.

Suddenly a Rebel counterattack led by a hard-charging cavalry swept over the Union flank, putting the army to flight. Even to untrained eyes the implications were obvious; the serene picnic ground was about to become a battle zone. Mass confusion erupted as the spectators fled, just moments before the Confederate wave washed over the hill. The entertainment was over. The battle was upon them.

The picnickers discovered something about war that day. You can't be close to it and safe from it at the same time. Only the naïve think they can stand on the sidelines of warfare and merely be entertained. When war enters the scene, everything it touches becomes a battlefield.

In chapter one, we learned about the central importance of having an accurate, biblical theology. In chapter two, we reviewed a core truth of that theology: that each of us is in fact the worst of sinners. In this chapter and the next, we want to understand this thing called sin a little better, examining its nature and learning how we tend to respond to it. After all, when you're the worst of sinners, it pays to know a few things about how sin actually works.

That's why I started this chapter with a battle. The nature of sin, you see, is war. Sin creates war—war with God, war with others, and war within yourself. Now in marriage, what do you have? Two sinners, each with the potential for war constantly lurking within them. Marriage, after all, is just life in a particularly concentrated form. Is it any wonder, then, that just as war overran the shocked and clueless picnickers at the Battle of Bull Run, the war of sin can sometimes engulf us when we least expect it?

Unlike the picnickers, however, this war of sin is one over which we do have some control. And when faced with sin's assault, what we should do depends on what kind of battle confronts us. When we are first tempted to sin—for example, tempted to become angry with a spouse—the battle is within, and we must go on the offensive: our goal is to defeat the sin, to not let it break out. Should we fail at this, and sin breaks out of our hearts into the larger battlefield of our marriages, we are called to be peacemakers: our goal is to end the fighting.[2]

Have you seen that you are the worst of sinners? In this chapter we will learn more about the warlike nature of our sin. Certainly, the New Testament Epistles assume the active, warmongering presence of sin in believers. Thankfully, however, they also provide both instruction and hope for how to battle that sin. The benefits of the new birth—the pardon of our sins and our relationship with Christ—do not remove us from the battle. Instead, they guarantee our victory! Informed by the Word of God, and empowered by the Holy Spirit, you can make your battles fewer, shorter, and not merely less harmful, but actually redemptive, allowing your marriage to steadily grow in sweetness.

Fighting for Freedom in the Clash of Desires

The members of the young church in Galatia were confused. Judaizers—the men who stalked Paul and sought to preach their own false version of the gospel—had crept in after his departure to draw these new believers back to formal religious practices rooted in Old Testament law. Paul would have none of it. His letter to the Galatians is his eloquent and impassioned defense of justification through grace by faith in the atoning sacrifice of Jesus Christ.

> For through the law I died to the law, so that I might live to God. I have been crucified with Christ. It is no longer I who live, but Christ who lives in me. And the life I now live in the flesh I live by faith in the Son of God, who loved me and gave himself for me. I do not nullify the grace of God, for if justifi-

cation were through the law, then Christ died for no purpose (Galatians 2:19–21).

In the letter we learn something wonderful. Those who are in Christ through faith in the gospel are truly free in Christ—free from the burden of trying to justify themselves by obeying Old Testament law (Galatians 5:1). I'm thankful that Paul, who understood so much about the sinfulness of his own heart, anticipated where the Galatians (and you and I) might go with that freedom. No longer bound by the burden of religious performance, we are apt to interpret our freedom as a license for ungodliness. Therefore Paul warned, "For you were called to freedom, brothers. Only do not use your freedom as an opportunity for the flesh, but through love serve one another" (Galatians 5:13).

Paul does not want us to remain under the tyranny of the law. Nor does he want us to abuse our liberty in Christ by embracing sin. His solution to both errors is the same. We must fight for freedom—freedom in Christ and because of Christ. See how clear Paul is about the conflict sin produces in our hearts, "For the desires of the flesh are against the Spirit, and the desires of the Spirit are against the flesh, for these are opposed to each other, to keep you from doing the things you want to do" (Galatians 5:17).

There it is. The sides in this war are not male versus female, husband versus wife, or controller versus enabler. It is a clash of desires—desires of the flesh against desires of the Spirit. It is trench warfare for supremacy of the human heart.

In Scripture, "the flesh" is another way of talking about the ongoing principle of sin. In fact, there are quite a few phrases used by Christians that all mean pretty much the same thing: "indwelling sin," "remaining sin," "the sin nature," "the flesh," and "the old man," to name a few. Some of these appear in Scripture and some don't, but every good spouse-theologian should understand that they all refer to the sin we each carry in our hearts. Whatever you call it, the goal of "the

flesh" is simple: "to keep you from doing the things you want
to do" (Galatians 5:17).

John Newton, author of the hymn "Amazing Grace," elo-
quently described his experience of Galatians 5, "I [do not
want] to be the sport and prey of wild, vain, foolish, and worse
imaginations; but this evil is present within me: my heart is
like a highway, like a city without walls or gates."[3]

Newton was expressing something that married people discover quickly, sometimes even before the honeymoon: there
is an evil "present within me." Although the penalty for my
sin has been paid by Christ, sin still remains, and it can keep
me from doing the things I want to do.

You realize, don't you, that there are desires within you
that organize to oppose the good things you want to do in
marriage? When we're not moving toward God, these desires
don't cause any trouble. But just try, for example, to plan a
regular prayer time with your spouse. Or seek to make yourself accountable in an area in which he or she would like you
to grow. How about when you start to confess a "small" sin,
and suddenly you want to point out the really "big" sin your
spouse dumped on you last week? Your warring, sinful desires
come out swinging. Why? Because their purpose is to keep
you from doing the things you want to do for God.

Despite the clarity of Paul's statement, married people sometimes assume that the cause of some of their wrong behavior
is their spouse. They may even try to justify sinful words and
deeds on that basis.

This is how it works (trust me, I know). Here I sit, just a
plain ole' loveable bundle of neutrality and noble-heartedness,
minding my own business, when my wife says or does something which, from my unassailable vantage point, clearly
crosses a line. Acting swiftly and efficiently as a judge and
jury of one, I evaluate her behavior as obviously sinful. Hers
is a transgression that demands my just but resolute response.
In order to deal swiftly with any violation of my emotional air

space or risk a breach of my personal security, I must expose her sin plainly and condemn it openly. If this creates a negative impact on my wife—the clear aggressor in my mind—well, a "stern" response from me is unfortunate but necessary to maintain the peace. In fact, I'm simply engaged in an act of leadership; perhaps she'll learn a lesson for the future.

Yes, it feels right, doesn't it—it seems so clear. But it's just my sinful flesh doing what it does best: making war against the Spirit and, in this case, against Kimm as well.

Kimm tells me that she can feel a similar soul skirmish when her desires collide with my legitimate leadership. Ladies, can you relate? Should your husband suggest drawing a warm bath with fragrant bubbles for you, marriage is suddenly bliss, just short of Eden. But what happens when that same leadership interferes with your plans? Do the words, "Dear, could you . . . " become his fingernails on the chalkboard of your agenda for the day?

For a busy wife with a full life, the unexpected input or leadership of a husband can seem like an ambush on her priorities. Kimm often has a plan for the day, with a lot to do. That plan reflects her sincere desire to serve the best interests of our marriage and family. But if my request threatens to restructure her day or week, altering her carefully arranged schedule, that noble desire can quickly become a subtle craving to manage and control her life on her own terms. Suddenly my "Honey, would you . . ." becomes a suggestion grenade that sets off a battle within her. She doesn't want a Spirit/flesh battle at that moment, but she gets it.

If blaming your spouse for actually causing your own sin sounds maybe just a little suspect, how much stranger is it to blame the marriage *itself*? Is it just me, or do we all do that sometimes?

"I'm fine when I'm at work," a spouse might say. "It's not until I get home that the battle begins." How easy it is to use the phrase, "We're having marriage problems," as if the marriage created them.

"Hey, bro, can you pray for me? My marriage is having some problems (or stranger still, some "issues"). Oh, *me?* No, I'm fine. Just gotta deal with these *marriage problems*, you know what I mean?"

This whole idea of seeing God, yourself, and your marriage for what they truly are is all about clear, biblical thinking. Locating the source of your marriage problems *in* your marriage is like saying the Battle of Bull Run was caused by some really troubled farmland. The battle was fought *on* farmland, but its cause lay elsewhere.

So How Did This Fight Get Started?

The cause of our marriage battles, friends, is neither our marriage nor our spouse. It's the sin in our hearts—entirely, totally, exclusively, without exception. This is taught clearly and consistently in Scripture, from the first sin to the final judgment. In addressing the futile attempts by the Pharisees to treat sin as something "out there," Jesus offers a penetrating and fully sufficient diagnosis of our root problem.

> But what comes out of the mouth proceeds from the heart, and this defiles a person. For out of the heart come evil thoughts, murder, adultery, sexual immorality, theft, false witness, slander. These are what defile a person.
>
> (Matthew 15:18–20a)

James takes this fundamental principle of human nature and drives it home, applying it to our personal relationships.

> What causes quarrels and what causes fights among you? Is it not this, that your passions are at war within you? You desire and do not have, so you murder. You covet and cannot obtain, so you fight and quarrel. You do not have, because you do not

ask. You ask and do not receive, because you ask wrongly, to spend it on your passions (James 4:1–3).

Simple, isn't it? Whatever shows up in my words or deeds comes from one place: my heart. God loves us so much he doesn't leave us looking for answers to the perplexing questions and challenges of marriage. The problem is not around us or outside of us. The problem is the "great opposition" within us.

G. K. Chesterton once responded to a newspaper article inviting readers all over the globe to answer the age-old question, "What's wrong with the world?"

His reply was brief and to the point, "I am."[4]

What's the greatest problem in my marriage? I am.

The Fog of War

Have you heard the phrase "the fog of war"? It's something that happens in the midst of battle—everything seems chaotic and nothing makes any sense. In the fog of war people do things that are completely out of character, things they would have sworn they could never do. The war between the flesh and Spirit can seem like that—we're just tossed to and fro by whatever impulse is strongest in the moment. And in those times we can do and say things we never thought possible. What drives us to take actions we regret? Consider the Apostle Paul's report from the front lines in Romans 7.

> So I find it to be a law that when I want to do right, evil lies close at hand. For I delight in the law of God, in my inner being, but I see in my members another law *waging war against the law of my mind* and *making me captive to the law of sin* that dwells in my members (Romans 7:22–23, emphasis added).

Paul discovered that sin has a purpose, an intent. He found a law, an "operating system" of sorts (for all you computer types) constantly at work within him. Paul said, "Part of me delights in God's law, but I see another law attempting to take me captive." Have you ever heard yourself or your spouse say:

"I can't believe I did that!"
"Where did that come from?"
"That's just not like me!"

Paul can relate. He calls it the law of sin at work. This law specifically opposes our desires for God, even the law of God being written on our hearts. The law of sin wants to take you captive to sin, and despite your assurance of salvation in Christ, this is serious stuff. Any sin can become enslaving. All sin does damage, which can be complex and long-lasting. We really do reap what we sow, and our battles have actual consequences. They are not war-games, but war itself.

Welcome to reality.

R. C. Sproul writes, "In one sense, life doesn't begin to get complicated until one becomes a Christian. When we are born of the Spirit we are born anew into a fierce struggle between the old man and the new man."[5] Are you a Christian? Are you married? You are new man *and* old man; woman of the Spirit *and* woman of the flesh. Right inside your own heart, you are in a battle.

I was converted twenty-six years ago and I still have the "law of sin" at work in my body. Now, don't be thrown by the word "law." It doesn't mean we are under the reign of sin or must continually atone for our sin. All atonement for all our sins for all time was accomplished for us by our wonderful Savior at the cross! But there still remains the powerful, active influence of sin within us. It is presented as a "law" because that is how it operates within us—it seeks to command and subdue us; it insists upon adherence; it targets our desire to do anything holy.

Let's say I'm driving home from a full day at work, looking forward to dinner on the table, a big smooch from my wife, and serenity in my house. My comforts are rarely a threat to the law of sin. However, suppose that the second or third thing Kimm says to me is, "We need to talk about what happened today . . ." and she's using the tone of voice that tells me there is a kid around, somewhere, guilty of something.

I know the right thing to do. I understand my responsibility to lead my family. I comprehend the gravity of the situation. I even grasp the wisdom of addressing things as soon as possible. But the law of sin engages at the point of decision. It wants me to do anything *except* the right thing. So it sets forth a much more appealing plan: Cast a deep, "Oh, the burdens of leadership" sigh toward my wife, bark out some general rebuke to whichever child is closest, and retreat to the internet for an update on *anything* happening *outside* my home.

What do I do when the law of sin gives me such a command? In the middle of an argument, when you *know* you're wrong, what stops you from simply saying, "Okay, you're right, I'm sorry"? The law of sin.

What do you imagine is the biggest factor keeping you from having a consistent devotional life? Yup, the law of sin.

When you know your marriage could use an investment in romance, why don't you make the effort? Once again, the law of sin.

Usually we are experts at finding the law of sin at work in our spouses, but not so sharp at noticing its activity in us. The law of sin can feel very much like simply "who we are," or "the way we're wired." After all, the commands of this law do come from inside us. But every married man or woman must be able to say with Paul, "So I find it to be a law that when I want to do right, evil lies close at hand" (Romans 7:22).

Where we were once citizens of sin's kingdom of darkness, now because of the finished work of Christ on the cross, we are citizens of God's kingdom of light. Each of those kingdoms has different laws for the citizens to obey. Becoming citizens of the kingdom of light guarantees our ultimate destination.

Yet, between now and then, sin can turn our hearts into a pretty effective fog machine.

The Betrayal of Sin

There are three things about the nature of sin that enable it to generate such a dense fog: sin is crafty, it is alluring, and it is treacherous.

Sin Is Crafty

Sin is crafty. It is inherently deceitful. The ultimate spiritual con game, sin stays in the shadows as it tries to control and take us captive. But unlike a con man who merely wants to separate us from our money, sin wants to separate us from God himself. Through its lies, sin presses us toward adopting a false perspective on our relationship with God.

We *depend on God* for our very lives. He is our benevolent provider of all good things, our wise and loving Father who has our best interest at heart. But sin would have us see God as *accountable to us* for our wants. This makes God into some magical genie whose only job is to make right whatever is currently bugging us, or a moody, petty despot whose unwillingness or inability to meet our needs is the source of our problems.

Although we have been *blessed* by God, sin would have us think of ourselves as *victimized* by God. That's how sin works now. That's how it worked "in the beginning."

Sin Is Alluring

In Genesis 3, the serpent begins to engage the woman, asking, "What did God tell you?" When she answers, the serpent unveils his true hostility toward God by contradicting God's word and distorting his character. "But the serpent said to the woman, 'You will not surely die. For God knows that when you eat of it your eyes will be opened, and you will be like God, knowing good and evil'" (Genesis 3:4–5).

Let me interpret this in sin-speak, "Don't be silly, Eve. You're not going to die. God knows what happens if you eat the fruit—you'll become like God . . . *and he fears that*! In fact, God trembles before the potential of a self-actualized, godlike human being. That's why he wants to keep you from eating from the tree. In fact, here's the real stunner, Eve: God is withholding from you! You're suffering a grave injustice . . . come on, Eve, you have rights!"

Let's go to instant replay. In the course of that one conversation, Adam and Eve started down a long and hazardous road. She went from being an accountable individual before a loving God to being a victim of an insecure God who was pathetically threatened by her autonomy. Adam was completely left out of the discussion between Eve and the serpent. Through its gentle coaxing, sin delivered the first couple—just like it delivers us—to an utterly insane conclusion: that the God who made us and holds every breath and every moment is not to be trusted!

Sin Betrays Us

When we see sin as crafty and alluring, the fog of war clears and the destruction, loss, and futility that sin creates can be plainly seen. Thomas Watson wrote, "Sin first courts, and then kills . . . Whoever sin kills, it betrays."[6] Here, "betray" means using a relationship of trust to deliver someone into the hands of an enemy. It's the ultimate bait-and-switch, a promise of blessing that in the end delivers a curse. Watson was looking at the same spiritual reality Paul had seen when he wrote in Romans 7:24, "Wretched man that I am! Who will deliver me from this body of death?"

Human beings are hardly ever capable of an anger that is completely holy. We nearly always manage to mix in a heaping teaspoon of self-righteousness. But when we really understand the malicious subtleties by which sin continually seeks to betray us, I think we can come pretty close. If we see that sin's betrayal of us is the biggest problem in our marriage, it can evoke, if not a perfectly holy anger, at least an indignant courage. And that's an emotion that comes in very handy on a battlefield.

Dancing on the Field of Victory

Friends, we *must* fight the battle with sin. If we don't, it *will* overrun us. But here's a promise that makes all the difference: By the cross of Christ the battle has already been won! Listen to the battle cry of Romans 8:

> There is therefore now no condemnation for those who are in Christ Jesus. For the law of the Spirit of life has set you free in Christ Jesus from the law of sin and death. For God has done what the law, weakened by the flesh, could not do. By sending his own Son in the likeness of sinful flesh and for sin, he condemned sin in the flesh, in order that the righteous requirement of the law might be fulfilled in us, who walk not according to the flesh but according to the Spirit.
>
> (Romans 8:1–4)

What does this mean for us in our battle with the flesh? It means that no matter how defeated we feel in the battle, we are overcomers because of two amazing expressions of the grace of God. We stand *forgiven in God's court* because of the atoning sacrifice of Christ—God no longer views us in relationship to our sin. And we are welcomed as *righteous in God's house* because of the imputed righteousness of Christ! ("Imputed" means that God counts the righteousness of Jesus as our own.)

God sees you as more than a forgiven sinner. He sees you as a holy person. Even though the power of sin continues to operate within you, its reign has been broken and God no longer sees you in reference to it. Please understand this: No matter how intense your battle with sin may rage, you fight as a forgiven sinner. You fight on the side of God, and God always wins in the end!

How does this relationship with God affect the battle? In the Romans 8 passage above, Paul indicates that the Holy Spirit himself works on our behalf as we walk "according to the Spirit." This echoes language that Paul used in Galatians 5, where the picture is of contrasting power—the fruit of the Spirit overcoming the works of the flesh (vss. 18–25). In Romans, the picture is of contrasting laws—the law of sin overcome by the law of the Spirit. In either case the truth is the same—a life set free from tyranny to sin and a heart increasingly conformed to the rule of Christ.

Marriage is joined upon a field of great spiritual battles. But it rests within a war that is already won. Our real opponent is not on the opposite side of the bed, but within our hearts. Our enemy is the desires of our flesh that oppose the desires of the Spirit. This is the fiercest and only true enemy of our marriage. We must know this enemy well.

This stunning discovery of the true nature of indwelling sin is not the end of our marriage battles, but it is an important beginning. It is the beginning of a new joy in our Savior and fresh delight in our spouses. It means there are no lost causes or hopeless conflicts. Each day is a day of new mercy and power to confess, love, forgive, and restore. Even better, marriage battles are no longer merely something to fight our way through, hoping we can come out on the other side with the relationship still intact. Instead, even our conflicts have redemptive possibilities because the war with sin is won in Christ, by the grace and power of our Sovereign God.

But as I said, the knowledge gained thus far in this book is just the beginning. Now that we know how sin behaves *toward us*, we need to learn, in the next chapter, how we often respond *to it*. For it is our responses to the law of sin that determine the outcome of any given battle.

We opened up this chapter talking about the Battle of Bull Run during the Civil War. That battle took place on a farm owned by a man named Wilmer McLean. After the battle was over, Wilmer decided he was a little too close to the action, so he moved himself as far away as he could—down to a little rural village in southern Virginia. Four years of war passed by and Wilmer lived in relative peace–until April 1865, when the war-ravaged armies of both General Grant and General Lee found themselves facing off once again, just a few hundred yards from Wilmer McLean's refuge in Appomattox, Virginia. Fortunately for Wilmer, and for the rest of the country, rather than slug it out one more time, the opposing forces made peace.

I don't know if Wilmer was a Christian, but I can't escape taking a couple of lessons from his odyssey. First, no matter how hard you try, you'll never be able to really avoid the war with sin this side of heaven. But even more profoundly, the end of war is meant to be peace. As we fight this battle within, and help our spouse in the fight, we have confidence that one day it will end, and the peace, which right now guards us in Christ, will be ours fully and for eternity.

Chapter Four

Taking it Out for a Spin

A Test Drive for Your Doctrine

*W*hat's the point of sitting here gunning the engine if we're not going anywhere?" The question seemed inspired at the moment. In retrospect, I think I was briefly possessed.

Terry, my thirteen-year-old buddy, had decided it would impress the neighborhood kids to get his brother's car keys, start the souped-up Chrysler, and sit there in the driveway revving the engine. I joined him as co-pilot since I was only twelve and far too young for the awesome responsibility of revving. Smoke billowed from the tailpipe as Terry perched behind the wheel punching the accelerator. The plan worked, causing quite a commotion. Kids gathered from as far away as Canada to see what was going on.

That's when the question formed in my mind. I probably should have *left* it as a question, but it just seemed pointless to stay parked in this awesome machine that was so ready to roll. My hand slowly reached for the gearshift.

Terry was oblivious. He was waving to the growing group of kids, a smile of triumph spread across his face. In the world of kid-dom, this was the equivalent of winning a NASCAR race. Little did he know that the race hadn't actually begun.

With split-second timing, I jerked the gearshift into drive at the exact moment he punched the accelerator. That's when I discovered two things. This Chrysler had pick-up! And Terry had never learned about brakes.

Fortunately, panic worked in our favor as Terry instinctively adopted the crash posture, a kind of seated fetal position. Somehow the car slipped out of gear and we gradually coasted to a stop without hitting a single house, tree, or person. No real harm done, we thought . . . until we got out of the car and faced a sea of stern parental faces. Certainly they would understand how pointless it is to just sit in a car like that but not put it in drive?

They didn't.

Put it in Drive

What compels two adolescent boys to act in such an audacious (or reckless, depending on your point of view) manner? Teenagers don't want to sit still. They want to put life in gear. And there's something of that restless desire in our relationship with God. God's grace at work in us compels us to not just sit behind the steering wheel, but put what we know into gear. When God saves us, we are drawn to unfamiliar things—to holiness, truth, the Scriptures, and God's amazing love. As we learn more, though, we have a desire to act on what we know and believe about God.

But how do we do this? How do we put our knowledge of God into gear—specifically into gear for our marriage? Biblically speaking, putting theology into gear means driving onto the road of wisdom. Wisdom in the Bible isn't some mystical knowledge or simple street savvy. It's the life and decisions of someone rightly related to God. It's applying what we know is true. Theologian Graham Goldsworthy says,

> . . . [Wisdom] is not primarily a function of how clever we are, nor of how much information we have managed to cram into our minds. Rather it is a moral choice to be independent of God or to be subject to him in our thinking as well as our doing.[1]

The way of wisdom is open for all who have believed the gospel, because Christ himself is our wisdom (1 Corinthians 1:30). That's why we can confidently ask for wisdom, and expect God to grant it to us (James 1:5). This freeway is open to us because of the gospel. Wisdom for our marriages then, is not found in "how to" books, or in formulas for success. It is found in putting our beliefs into gear and heading down the road of wisdom with God behind the wheel.

So why sit around gunning the engine on our theology of sin unless we're going to put this machine into drive? Why have a powerful car that never leaves the garage? Progress comes when we slip our theology into gear and find out what it can do. Let me offer four roads you can practice on. I'm confident if you can drive on these roads, you can get about anywhere you need to go in your marriage.

First Gear: In Humility, Suspect Yourself First

It is very important in our Christian lives to be suspicious of any claims to righteousness we bring to our relationship with God. It is in Christ alone, and in his merit alone, that we trust. True humility is living confident in Christ's righteousness, and suspicious of our own.

The word "suspicion" often gets a bad rap. An ominous cloud hangs over it—it's nearly always negative. People in custody are suspicious. Gangs at night are suspicious. Smiling children around empty cookie jars are suspicious. Christians should not be suspicious. Or should we?

Let's backtrack down the road of your last conflict. She said something; he did something. Things went wrong—happens all the time. When we seek to address difficulties in our marriage, does a humble suspicion of our hearts influence our assumptions and approach?

This may be a shocker, but we *should* be suspicious . . . selectively, permanently, and internally. As the worst of sinners, in the day-to-day conflicts of marriage, I should be *primarily* suspicious and *regularly* suspicious *of myself!* To be suspicious of my own heart is to acknowledge two things: that my heart has a central role in my behavior, and that my heart has a permanent tendency to oppose God and his ways.

This is an area where you have to train yourself. The humility of a healthy self-suspicion definitely does not come naturally. It's always a low road—safe and secure, but not exactly the scenic highway. And sadly, it's often the less-traveled road in marriage.

When you're in a conflict with your spouse, or evaluating a past conflict, have you ever said (aloud or to yourself), "God knows my heart in this situation"? Was that a comforting or reassuring thought? Did you imagine that a divine examination of your deepest motives and desires would uncover nothing but the purest and most Christ-like intentions? If so, you were on a dangerous stretch of road with no guardrail at all, and probably well on your way to hurtling down into the bottomless canyon of self-deception. We're talking crash and burn. But to live suspicious of your heart's motivations, that's safe spiritual driving.

Many marriage problems could move toward resolution if husband and wife actually lived as if they were "sinners" who said, "I do." Sinners who are humble are growing more knowledgeable about their hearts. In doing so, they are discovering what's really going on—that the ability to claim righteousness apart from Christ undermines the truth of the gospel. Why not better acknowledge what the cross says about you and relish the truth that J. I. Packer so vividly states, "Our best works are shot through with sin and contain something for which we need to be forgiven."[2] Sound bleak? It sure does. But it is the gateway to the safe, low road of humility.

Second Gear: In Integrity, Inspect Yourself

Perhaps you have heard the story about the backwoods man taking his family to the big city for the first time. Walking the streets, mesmerized by the great skyscrapers, the family follows a crowd through some strange, slowly spinning glass doors. As they emerge into a huge indoor area, the mother and a daughter stop to marvel at a gliding silver staircase. The father and son move further into the building, and in a few moments they're standing in front of a large wall filled with several pairs of shiny metal doors, with lighted buttons next to each one.

As they gaze at some blinking numbers above the doors, a bedraggled old woman with a red shopping bag approaches the set of doors nearest them. As if by magic the doors slide apart, revealing a small, empty, wood-paneled room. The woman steps in and the doors slide closed behind her. The family stands transfixed: What's happening in there? Why would she want to go into such a tiny room? After a minute or so the doors magically open again. Out steps a beautiful, energetic woman who brushes past them, red shopping bag in hand.

Without taking his eyes off the elevator, the father leans down and whispers to his boy, "Son, go get your mother."

Apart from the amusement value, I like this story because it speaks to a common tendency we all have: we often want to fix our marriage problems by "fixing" our spouses. Later in this book we'll examine more closely what to do when love requires that we address the sins of our spouses. But in marriage that's not the place to *begin*. Scripture does not give me permission to make the sins of my spouse my first priority. I need to slow down, exercise the humility of self-suspicion, and inspect my own heart first.

Consider the words of Christ on how we should address the sin of another person.

> How can you say to your brother, "Let me take the speck out of your eye," when there is the log in your own eye? You hypocrite, first take the log out of your own eye, and then you will see clearly to take the speck out of your brother's eye.
>
> (Matthew 7:3–5)

Imagine a husband, railroad tie protruding from his face, attempting to remove a dust particle from his wife's eye. He will have whacked her silly long before he can address her speck. Just approaching her brings pain.

In using the image of logs and specks, Jesus reveals this approach as wrong, ineffective (to put it mildly), and absurd. When our goal is to address someone else's sin, Jesus tells us, *our own sin* must loom large in our sight. It must be, by far, the primary and more significant issue. What is striking is his use of the word "hypocrite" to describe those who are speck focused. Why such a seemingly harsh assessment? It has to do with the blatancy of the log. Jesus is saying that to ignore the "obvious" log in favor of the not-so-obvious speck is not simply wrong, it is hypocrisy. In other words, it lacks integrity to ignore a major problem to deal with something trivial, simply because that's where you prefer to focus.

Let's say you and your spouse have recently had a conflict to which both of you contributed some sin (this, by the way, probably describes every conflict you have ever experienced!). What would happen if you evaluated that conflict in light of this passage, *and your spouse did too?*

66

What if, to you, the log (not the speck) was yours . . . and to your spouse the log (not the speck) was his or hers? Would one of you be wrong? Would that be a misapplication of this passage? I don't think so. I think it's exactly what is supposed to happen!

Jesus is not concerned here with which of you is *more at fault* in a particular instance. His emphasis is your *focus*, what you find to be the *most obvious fact* to you whenever sin is in view. He's calling for the inspection to begin with me. In light of who we are compared to God, and because of the reality of remaining sin, it is nothing more than basic integrity to consider our sin before we consider the sin of our spouse. To do otherwise lacks integrity. It's hypocritical.

Wisdom connects integrity to humility in a pretty simple way. If you *suspect* yourself (humility), you are more likely to *inspect* yourself first (integrity). This road feels narrow to us, because we are constantly looking for an off-ramp to focus on the sins of someone else. But if we stay on it, we can be confident that it will take us where Jesus wants us to go. So how do we stay on the narrow road of integrity?

Make sure you suspect and inspect the accuracy of your perceptions. When a conflict emerges, is your sense of where your spouse has sinned clear, crisp, and obvious? Are you looking forward to that moment when you can deliver the telling line, "Honey, if you're looking at this objectively, you have to admit your sin"? Beware the off-ramp of pride.

None of us are omniscient. Nor are we Old Testament prophets pronouncing judgment. We are saints who are still sinners. We only know in part (1 Corinthians 13:12), and since we cannot see the complete picture, we just might be wrong.

Okay, maybe you think you *are* able to be more objective than your spouse. But even if that's true, your objectivity is itself tainted by sin. You must bring to these conversations an awareness of your own sinful drives and desires that is *more* tangible and *more* vivid than your awareness of your spouse's sin. This will lower your irritation and soften your tone of voice.

Also, avoid the off-ramp of self-righteousness. Integrity calls you to suspect and inspect your motives. Are you really doing this to bless, encourage, and help your spouse? Or do you actually have a strong interest in chalking up a few points for the home team? Do you hope to be proven right? To be vindicated? To emerge as spiritually superior? Who are you intending to serve—your spouse or yourself?

So if you find yourself on a speck hunt in your marriage, it's probably because your suspicions are misdirected and you're inspecting the wrong spouse. Marriages flourish when both partners learn to stay on the narrow road of integrity. I want to suspect and inspect my own heart first. That is where I will discover, not only the most obvious sin, but the only sin I can directly change.

Third Gear: Admit that Circumstances Only Reveal Existing Sin

There is a lot of talk these days about the need for honesty in marriage. Unfortunately, what's being advocated looks more like a license to verbally unload on our spouse whatever we're "feeling" for the sake of "emotional honesty." Sadly, this approach in practice typically produces great hurt and offense. Though honesty is essential in marriage, we must be able to build trust and resolve offenses. The problem is not with the honesty itself, but in the intent of a person's honest words.

As we have already learned, our problems come from how our hearts engage with the circumstances around us. If we are applying gospel wisdom, we see the hand of God in every situation, working for our ultimate good. In marriage, this means that God will create opportunities to reveal and then deal with sin that keeps us from living in wisdom.

68

After I was saved, and before I was married, I lived under the mad, undaunted delusion that I was spiritually mature. Mine was a rich and largely imaginary kind of holiness. If ignorance is bliss, I was in permanent ecstasy. The infrequent examinations of my seemingly innocent heart revealed little need for improvement. I lived expecting that at any moment God might send chariots to carry me to heaven, Elijah-like. Talk about a guy in need of the doctrine of sin.

Then it happened. I got married and became a blame-shifter.

John Bettler has said, "Your spouse always hooks your idol." (Where were you twenty-five years ago, Dr. Bettler?) But marriage didn't simply hook my idols; it hoisted them six feet in the air and towed them around the house. I can't tell you how many times I thought, "I never had these problems before. This must be my wife's fault." The truth is, I'd always been a blameshifter—it's just that after getting married there were so many more good opportunities to express this fault!

Personally, I locate the blame for my blameshifting in my extended family history: Adam started it. "Yeah Lord, it's this woman you gave me" (Genesis 3:12, paraphrased). Like me, I bet a lot of your blameshifting in marriage sounds like Adam's.

"It's this husband you gave me."

"It's her nagging."

"It's his rudeness."

"It's this person so unlike me!"

Thoughts like these dump us into the same place they dumped Adam all those years ago—the sewer of self-justification. To try to justify ourselves is to deny our guilt before God. But that's a futile effort. Blameshifting will fool some of the people some of the time, but it will never fool God any of the time.

Blameshifting is a little different from something we discussed earlier—which is to think of my spouse or my marriage as actually *causing* conflicts (since the only true cause is sin). Blame-shifting is what I do when I basically *know* I'm guilty and am just trying to convince myself or someone else that maybe I'm not.

You see, your wicked heart and mine are amazingly similar. They both crave vindication. They want to insist that something else made us sin . . . something outside of us . . . beyond our control. Aha—our circumstances!

The road of honesty is a straight road—it cuts straight through to our hearts. If you've ever driven out west on one of those long desert roads, one thing you'll notice is that the scenery all starts looking familiar. You realize that the road wasn't built for touring, it was built to get you where you need to go. The straight road of honesty has that feel. You drive down it and you see the same heart temptations you've always seen, the same ruts of thinking that get you sidetracked. Honesty forces us to deal with the familiar indwelling sin of our lives in a straightforward way. And the destination is always the same—the foot of the cross where our sin has been atoned for and where Christ, our wisdom, is ready to help in time of need.

Not long ago, my son started the lawnmower with the oil cap loose. Once the engine heated up, the poor kid struck oil. And it was a geyser! Since I don't change the oil often (read: never), a slimy black sludge erupted from the engine, covering the lawnmower, my son, and everything within a six-foot radius. (It's because of stuff like this that I don't cut grass.)

This might be a helpful illustration for understanding the operation of remaining sin. Original sin filled the "engine" of our hearts with the "oil" of depravity—dark, greasy, and staining everything it touches. Circumstances come along and heat the engine. When the engine is hot—when events in our lives test our hearts by stirring anger, lust, greed, etc.—whatever is in the engine spews out. The heat (the circumstances) did not fill the engine with oil, it simply revealed what was in the engine.

Experienced any heat lately?

Husbands, you jump in the car only to find (sigh) that the gas gauge you've reminded your wife about (hmmff) is on empty again (seethe). What's happening? Has your spouse sinned against you? Maybe, or maybe not. The complaint and contempt that's filling your mind—is that *caused* by a gas gauge or by your wife? No, it's simply showing you the impatience that was already in the engine of your heart. The heat just stirred it up and made it obvious.

Wives, for the hundredth time (eyes roll) he has walked up the steps (groan) without touching the pile of clothes that obviously needs to be taken upstairs (disgusted gaze). What's happening as the accusation, "at least he's consistent at being lazy," slips out under your breath? The engine's heating, the cap is loose, and an oil spill is on its way!

Have you ever considered why there are no accounts of Jesus slamming a door in angry frustration or inflicting the "silent treatment" on someone who hurt him? Why didn't Jesus get irritated or bitter or hostile? The simple but astounding answer is that when his engine was heated by circumstances, what was in his heart came out: love, mercy, compassion, kindness. Christ didn't respond sinfully to the circumstances in his life—even an undeserved, humiliating, torturous death—because the engine of his heart was pure. What was in his heart spilled over. It was love!

Your spouse was a strategic choice made by a wise and loving God. Selected by him, for you, from the beginning of the world, your spouse is an essential part of God's rescue mission for your life. Often a spouse plays his or her part by raising the engine temperature and heating the oil. But if we're wisely honest we will realize that God is behind it all, revealing the familiar sin so that it might be overcome by amazing grace.

Fourth Gear: Focus on Undeserved Grace, Not Unmet Needs

Think about your last conflict. What caused it? If you answer, "My spouse is not giving me what I need!" you're not alone. Ask "marriage experts" how marriages unravel and many will start with unmet needs. Recently, the Sunday paper in our area did a review of new marriage books that tackled the question, "How can couples get along better?" Each author came to essentially the same conclusion: "By meeting emotional needs."[3]

In the twenty-first century, marriage is offered as nature's answer to our emotional deficits. Sadly, the church often parrots this dogma with a supposedly Christianized version of the same message.

But according to Scripture, the source of angry words, unforgiving looks, and cold shoulders is not unmet needs. It's unsatisfied desires. We discussed this briefly in chapter two. Let's return to that passage and unpack the treasure chest a bit more.

> What causes quarrels and what causes fights among you? Is it not this, that your passions are at war within you? You desire and do not have, so you murder. You covet and cannot obtain, so you fight and quarrel. You do not have, because you do not ask.
>
> (James 4:1–2)

Guess what? Your last heated exchange was not caused by an unsatisfied need; it was not "her lack of respect" or "his lack of affection." It was caused by renegade desires—"passions at war within us."

So is all this a question of what is an "actual need" and what is "only" a desire? While that's a valuable distinction, we must see that Scripture places the blame for conflict squarely on our passions—on *how much* I want something, *regardless of how "legitimate" that desire is*. If my desire is so strong

72

that I am tempted to sin, then the problem is entirely me. It's my desire, my sin, the grimy oil in my own heart erupting in response to the heat of circumstances.

With a sentence or two, James masterfully shifts our entire paradigm from something we're *missing* (an unmet need) to something we're *doing* (passionately desiring something we're not getting). Lurking beneath our unmet needs are desires demanding satisfaction. We "desire but do not have."

Can my words or behavior *tempt* my spouse to start or escalate a conflict? Of course. (And when I do that, I add my own sin to an already bad situation.) But there's nothing I can do to *cause* a sinful response in my spouse. The sin that emerges from a spouse's heart was already there.

I grew up in an ordered home. No, strike that. When socks are folded and arranged in their own drawer by color for easy visual reference, you've moved way beyond ordered. Kimm, on the other hand, grew up in a home where there were no sock drawers. I'm not sure how that worked. I regularly remind her that it's the people with organized sock drawers who run the world. She is quick to remind me that while this may be true, they don't actually enjoy it. That's when I shut up and go back to folding my socks.

Not surprisingly, some of the conflicts early in our marriage were about order. I was convinced that I needed order. My sock-drawer mentality applied to practically everything in my life. To me it was clearly a biological necessity, ranking right up there with vitamins, air, and really good lasagna. And I could make a great case for order. Beginning in Genesis, I could walk right through the Bible—creation, Numbers, the Temple, Corinth—the God of my Bible was the God of Order. If God was about order, and I was created in his image, then I needed order. Yep, my very soul depended on it.

Kimm was great. She would never attack order; she knows it's a good thing. But she would ask questions about why it was so important to me. Why does a disruption of order sometimes incite anger or anxiety in me? Over time, through the help of my patient wife and some faithful friends, I began to see that my need for order was really a sinful craving. This doesn't mean order itself is bad. But there was a kind of security and trust that I placed in the control that order facilitated. When that broke down, my cravings were agitated and my heart was exposed. The desire itself was not wrong. But it was a desire I had simply assumed should be met. It was a desire masquerading as a need—something I wanted tricked out as something I had to have. And when events in my marriage came between me and my demand for order, well, the socks went flying.

Needs are not wrong; we all have them. They exist as daily reminders that we were created as dependent beings, in fundamental need of God and his provision for our lives. But maintaining a distinction between genuine needs and those needs invented by a self-indulgent culture is essential for a healthy marriage.

Is it wrong to desire the gentle caress of a husband's hand or the kind words from a wife's tongue? Absolutely not. But even things that are good for a marriage can be corrupted if they are defined as needs. The problem is not that we desire—desire is completely natural; it's that our desires become juiced with steroids. Calvin called our desires "inordinate."[4]

It's not wrong to desire appropriate things like respect or affection from our spouses. But it is very tempting to justify demands by thinking of them as needs and then to punish one another if those needs are not satisfied. A needs-based marriage does not testify to God's glory; it is focused on personal demands competing for supremacy. Two people, preoccupied with manipulating each other to meet needs, can drive their marriage down the path of "irreconcilable differences." This is cultural language that simply acknowledges that a marriage can no longer carry the weight of demands understood as needs.

Perhaps though, the saddest part of driving down the road of unmet needs is where we end up. The road of unmet needs leads to nowhere. It is a forlorn, one-lane stretch of me. All it leads to is more of me. It's worse than a dead end—it's a circle that never ends.

But sinners who say "I do" have a different road to travel. It is the road of astonishing, undeserved grace—a grace so remarkable that it shows us the problem and then delivers the solution. Have you ever been on a scenic drive so beautiful that it was hard to keep your head from spinning from one vista to the next? The road of undeserved grace is like that. It is distractingly beautiful, because all of our true needs are met in breathtaking array in Christ. But it is a road of constant surprises, because we drive it with full awareness of our sin in light of the cross. How can such a road produce such joy? I think you'll begin to see better as we look ahead. So buckle up and let's put it in gear.

Chapter Five

Mercy Triumphs
Over Judgment

How to Sweeten the Days and Years

ordon and Emma met at a church function. She was an admirable young woman, and he was a fairly new pastor. Their wedding day seemed to be the launch of a godly couple into the promise of fruitful ministry in the decades ahead. But just a few days into their honeymoon, all of Emma's dreams for her life were crushed. Gordon made it clear that he didn't love Emma, and that he had married her simply because there were more opportunities for married pastors than single ones.

For forty years, through the birth of six children, and all the while functioning as a pastor, Gordon made no meaningful attempt to kindle love for his wife. Freely admitting to an adulterous affair that began after the birth of their fourth child, Gordon insisted he must remain married—divorce would derail his pastoral career. Marriage for Emma became a life of secret shame. She was relegated to sharing a room with their two daughters, while her husband stayed in a separate room, and their four sons in another.

This is part of the true story of a couple, now deceased, one of whom I knew personally. It is not, however, the end of their story. Theirs is an extreme case, perhaps the most severe example of long-term callous disregard I have ever encountered in a Christian marriage. But the story has an ending you might not expect. It may seem to be all about failure and loss. But it became something altogether different. It's a story all about mercy.

A Curious Command

Jesus had something to say to people in Emma's situation. Descending from the mountain after spending the entire night in prayer, Jesus brought with him twelve names. It was time to begin forming believers into disciples and disciples into a church. The men whose names the Lord carried in his heart would become his chief disciples, his closest companions, and (with one exception) the key leaders of the first church. Sometimes I wonder if, after seeing these guys in action, Jesus ever wanted to return to the mountain for new names—but Jesus wasn't looking back. Now was the time to spell out a code of conduct for these twelve and for all others whom the Savior would call. What would it mean to serve Christ? First came the Beatitudes—as Luke records it, four blessings packed with hope for the future, followed by four warnings to those as yet unaware of their need for a Savior. Then, in going to the heart of the matter, things got really interesting.

But I say to you who hear, Love your enemies, do good to those who hate you, bless those who curse you, pray for those who abuse you. To one who strikes you on the cheek, offer the other also, and from one who takes away your cloak do not withhold your tunic either. Give to everyone who begs from you, and from one who takes away your goods do not demand them back. And as you wish that others would do to you, do so to them. If you love those who love you, what benefit is that to you? For even sinners love those who love them. And if you do good to those who do good to you, what benefit is that to you? For even sinners do the same. And if you lend to those from whom you expect to receive, what credit is that to you? Even sinners lend to sinners, to get back the same amount. But love your enemies, and do good, and lend, expecting nothing in return, and your reward will be great, and you will be sons of the Most High, for he is kind to the ungrateful and the evil. Be merciful, even as your Father is merciful.

(Luke 6:27–36)

Consider who was listening to Jesus— peasants, fisherman, tax collectors, zealots, prostitutes—an assemblage of riffraff in the eyes of both the Roman occupiers and the Jewish religious authorities. People who were hated and cursed by others. People with real enemies. Now consider the commands the Lord gave to them: Love your enemies; do good to those who hate you; don't strike back; and lend freely to those who may never repay you.

Consider what in the world Christ was saying: He summarizes it right there in the final command. It's all about mercy.

Giving Shape to Mercy

Mercy is a unique, marvelous, exceptional word. God's mercy means his kindness, patience, and forgiveness toward us. It is his compassionate willingness to suffer for and with sinners for their ultimate good.

In the Bible, mercy weds the severe obligation of justice with the warmth of personal relationship. Mercy explains how a holy and loving God can relate to sinners without compromising who he is. God doesn't thump his chest and parade this attribute, as if it's unique to him but unattainable by us. He gives it to us freely, a gift to pass along. "Be merciful, even as your Father is merciful" (Luke 6:36).

Before we were Christians, we weren't neutral or ambivalent toward God, we were against God, we were his enemies (Romans 5:10), destined for wrath as willing followers of the devil himself (Ephesians 2:1–3). That's a pretty grim picture. But God chose to respond to us, his enemies, in love. That is mercy. That is the reality of the cross Christians have experienced. That is the example for us to follow.

This also raises some important questions for sinners who say "I do." Do you know God as a God of mercy? Do you see your spouse as God sees him or her—through eyes of mercy?

If your answer to either question is no, it is unlikely that your marriage is sweet. Mercy sweetens marriage. Where it is absent, two people flog one another over everything from failure to fix the faucet to phone bills. But where it is present, marriage grows sweeter and more delightful, even in the face of challenges, setbacks, and the persistent effects of our remaining sin.

Kimm loves coffee. Actually, she would say her desire sped past love years ago and now qualifies as an obsession. But I'm happy to say she's no trembling caffeine addict. She only drinks decaf. What she loves most about coffee is the taste and the experience—a warm cup and warm conversation to go with it. To me, that's still an obsession, even if it is an endearing one.

I'm more of a tea guy. My friends consider tea to be feminine, but I don't think hard enough in the morning to ask gender questions of my breakfast drink. I'm just glad to have the right shoes on the right feet. And I like my tea sweet. Splenda, Sweet'N Low, Equal . . . it doesn't matter. Just back up the truck and dump it in. A sweetener works its magic by taking what is bitter and making it sweet. Like the sweetener in my tea, mercy changes the flavor of relationships. Mercy sweetens the bitterness out of relationships—especially marriage. So just back up the truck and dump the mercy in.

Pass it Along

Have you ever thought that passing along God's mercy may be one of the main reasons you're married? Think about it like this: Marriage is a place where two sinners become so connected that all the masks come off. It's not only that we sometimes put on our best faces in public, it's that when we're married we see each other in all kinds of situations, including some very difficult ones. All the wonderful diversity (in this case, a polite word for our personal quirks, weaknesses, and sin patterns) that was kept refined and subdued before the wedding tumbles out of the closet after the honeymoon. We begin to see each other as we really are—raw, uncensored, and in Technicolor. If our eyes are open, we discover wonderful things about our spouses that we never knew were there. We also discover more of the other person's weaknesses. It's no wonder that Martin Luther called marriage "the school of character."[1] Without mercy, differences become divisive, sometimes even "irreconcilable." But deep, profound differences are the reality of every marriage. It's not the presence of differences but the absence of mercy that makes them irreconcilable. How many sinners who say "so long" would remain as lovers who said "I do" if they understood the place of mercy in marriage?

Last Christmas, Kimm received a friendship ball. That's a Christmas ornament filled with potpourri and other fragrant stuff guys don't tend to notice. My wife explained that a friendship ball is given as a gift, but it's expected that once enjoyed, it will be passed along. It is to be re-given. The point is not only to receive it but transfer it.

That's an example of what to do with mercy. It's to be received, enjoyed, celebrated . . . but then it must be passed along. The Father offered mercy to us so that we might share it. How do we become sharers of mercy? It doesn't happen by accident.

Mercy in Real-Time

Sweet marriages are built on mercy dispensed. A wife is locked in a cycle of complaining; a husband seems paralyzed by self-pity. Luke 6 changes how we approach them. Rather than using the old recipe (pour accusation into conversation, add a cup of defensiveness, stir with angry glances, heat at increasing volume, repeat often), we use the new organic recipe: Magnificent Mercy!

Mercy doesn't change the need to speak truth. It transforms our motivation from a desire to win battles to a desire to represent Christ. It takes me out of the center and puts Christ in the center. This requires mercy.

Mercy takes people who are capable of open warfare over toothpaste tubes and toilet seats, and enlarges their vision to include a Savior. Mercy confronts a sinner wrapped in self-pity and protected by pride and shows him the way out of the darkness into the light. Mercy inspires us to move beyond "the power and government of self-love" back to the nobler and benevolent principles of our new nature.[2]

We're not only sinners; we are also the objects of other people's sin. We have enemies, people who don't like us, who abuse us, who make unreasonable demands of us. People who treat us how they want to without consideration of our feelings. In Luke 6, Christ is relating some pretty distressing details about life.

For many reading this book, I can hear the question, "Yes, but Luke 6 hardly describes my marriage. After all, enemies don't get married. Men don't propose to women they hate. People who curse and abuse each other aren't typically gazing into each other's eyes and whispering "I do." What does this passage have to do with marriage?"

Everything—because Christ is showing the comprehensive reach of mercy. By addressing grievous scenarios, he is setting the bar for normal life. He is saying, "Okay, now on to mercy. Let's move right to the egregious cases—such as your enemies, those who hate and curse and strike and abuse you—because when you know how to deal with committed enemies, you'll know how to deal with occasional enemies. When you can extend mercy to the spiteful, violent, selfish, and wicked, you can extend it to those who annoy, ignore, or disappoint you."

Now before I go any further, I need to speak to a very specific situation—safety in an abusive marriage. There are situations where the violent or abusive behavior of a spouse (and let's be frank, this overwhelmingly applies to men) puts the safety of the other spouse or children at risk. In these cases, sadly occurring even in Christian homes, the need to separate an abuser from those he abuses is imperative, and is in fact an expression of mercy in the situation. It not only protects innocent parties, it mercifully gives a person trapped in violent sin the opportunity to face themselves, repent, and change. I know of men whose greatest expressions of thankfulness to God are because of how he arrested their lives with the interdicting mercy of a courageous spouse, friend, or pastor.

Mercy is given to be shared. And what it touches, it ultimately sweetens. We are to pass along what we have received from God—steadfast love, inexplicable kindness, overflowing compassion. We sinned against God and he responded with mercy. We are called to go and do the same.

Now, how about a practical look at how mercy works in the day-to-day?[3]

Mercy Before the Fact: Practice Kindness

One of the truly amazing things about God's mercy to us is that he sees *every* sinful action, motive, and thought we ever have, yet still relates to us in love. God loves sinners, simple as that, and certainly not because of the sin, but in spite of it. His love expresses itself in kindness toward sinners, and that kindness is meant to *lead us to* repentance (Romans 2:4). The phrase "lead us to" tells us his loving-kindness meets us prior to repentance and draws us forward. What a lavish demonstration of mercy toward those who, left to themselves, would flee from God!

The promise of mercy is traceable throughout the Old Testament. Indeed, God has always had a disposition of kindness toward us. Before Adam and Eve sinned, God had determined to express love and mercy toward his people. There's nothing about sin that has ever changed his mind or altered his plan. And that plan, of course, finds its ultimate fulfillment in Christ.

Notice that Luke 6 is not a call to discrete, isolated acts of mercy, but something much broader—to a merciful disposition of heart, to lovingkindness. Dwelling in the heart, lovingkindness preempts our sinful judgments. God doesn't just dispense mercy. He *is* merciful (Luke 6:36).

Such kindness expressed to us makes a claim upon us: We are called to continue in the kindness we have received (Romans 11:22). We don't wait to be sinned against and then try to respond with mercy. Rather, we adopt the posture of being willing to experience sin against us as part of building a God-glorifying marriage in a fallen world. Kindness says to our spouse, "I know you are a sinner like me and you will sin against me, just like I sin against you. But I refuse to live defensively with you. I'm going to live leaning in your direction with a merciful posture that your sin and weakness cannot erase."

How can you be kind knowing that there may be another sin against you right around the corner? Because kindness does not have its origins in you, but in God. It isn't a personality trait, it's a fruit of the Spirit (Galatians 5:22; Colossians 3:12) and an expression of biblical love (1 Corinthians 13:4). Kindness recognizes that God's mercies are new every morning (Lamentations 3:23). There is fresh grace for each failure for both the sinner and the one sinned against. And kindness is a posture of heart that flows out in actions—daily-life stuff that reprograms behavior in marriage away from self-focus to the redemptive purposes of God.

The faithful practice of lovingkindness sows experiences of grace into marriage. The coffee run for the husband working late, the mini-van washed and cleaned out for the busy mom, the intentional words of encouragement in an area of weakness—these are more than good manners or duties. They are kindnesses sown into the normal routine of life. They are the grace moments that we draw on in times of trial.

Mercy When Under Attack: Do Unto Others

In his book on ministry in personal relationships, Paul Tripp makes this sobering point:

In personal ministry, the sin of the person you are helping will eventually be revealed in your relationship. If you are ministering to an angry person, at some point that anger will be directed at you. If you are helping a person who struggles with trust, at some point she will distrust you. A manipulative person will seek to manipulate you. A depressed person will tell you he tried everything you've suggested and it didn't work. You can't stand next to a puddle without eventually being splashed by its mud.[4]

How muddy are you right now in your marriage? Are you being splashed by the sins of your spouse? How should you respond? Why not turn the question around? How much mud have you been slinging?

Have you ever wondered where to find the golden rule? It's there in Luke 6:31. As a young Presbyterian, I memorized it like this, "Do unto others as you would have them do unto you." The ESV translates it, "And as you wish that others would do to you, do so to them." Whatever the phrasing, the point is the same. Use how you want to be treated as the measure for how you treat others. Often the golden rule is understood as a way to keep from making enemies. But Jesus gives the golden rule specifically for situations where enemies have already come into the picture. It is his commanded response strategy when we come under attack.

Again, a response of actual mercy is only possible for sinners like you and me when we pass along the mercy we've received from God. But these are the responses that make all the difference over the life of a marriage. Here are some practical ways we can show mercy when under attack:

- Remind yourself that your greatest enemy is "the enemy within"—your own sin. We covered this in chapters two and three.
- When you're not in a conflict, ask each other the question, "What behavior of mine expresses anger or a lack of love for you?" Take your spouse's answer and attempt to do the opposite when you feel sinned against.
- Learn to love in the style of 1 Corinthians 13 by being "patient, kind, and not resentful." Resist being a defense attorney in your mind. Fire the "prosecuting attorney"

within—it's nothing but an expression of the sin of arrogance.

• Memorize and apply this wise advice from James, "Let every person be quick to hear, slow to speak, slow to anger; for the anger of man does not produce the righteousness that God requires" (James 1:19–20). Applying this one verse in the heat of conflict can have an amazing effect on where the conflict goes.

• Where patterns of sin are causing persistent problems, draw in the outside counsel of friends, pastors, etc. who can help you spot where chronic problems are occurring and provide accountability for responses of love.

Ideas like this will not eliminate conflict. But they are biblically sound strategies for responding to the heat of our spouse's sin in a way that doesn't just increase the temperature or complicate the process of resolution. One thing I've learned, if I can avert a two-hour argument with two minutes of mercy, that's a win for everybody involved.

Mercy After the Fact: Cover Sin

So here you are. She did that again. He said that again. While you are always aware of your own temptations, you've truly been trying to love with kindness and treat your spouse as you would want to be treated. You've been careful to try to please God in how you've responded. And yet once again it's happening, and what bad timing. You're walking into church—a little battle under the breath before he heads off to usher and she's off to children's ministry. Gotta look happy for the visitors and children. So you're in that awkward place where something isn't right but it can't be resolved. What do you do?

You could agree to pick it up later, which is always a great idea—but what if later can't happen for a couple of days? Is it really that big a deal to keep it in mind? You could take the time to work it out right now, inconveniencing others in the process. Do you just try to forget it, only to see it pop up in some future conflict? Do you file it away in "Things About My Spouse that Need to Change"? How about an exorcism?

Maybe you didn't know this, but the Bible gives you a special privilege in dealing with sin committed against you. It's called forbearance. It means that you can bring love into play in such a way that you can cut someone free from their sin against you—without them even knowing or acknowledging what they've done! Forbearance is an expression of mercy that can cover both the big sins of marital strife and the small sins of marital tension. And let's face it; small sins are the fuel for most marital blazes.

Let's be careful here. Forbearance doesn't mean we tuck sin away for another time. It's not a variation on patience, nor is it some Christianized, external "niceness" where you pretend nothing bothers you. It's not even a kind of ignoring the sin, in the sense of refusing to acknowledge it.

In forbearance, we know (or at least suspect) we have been sinned against, but we actually make a choice to overlook the offense and wipe the slate clean, extending a heart attitude of forgiveness and treating the (apparent) sin as if it never happened. Proverbs 19:11 tells us it is a "glory to overlook an offense." Forbearance is preemptive forgiveness, freely and genuinely bestowed.

Of course, righteousness often demands that we address the sin of another, even if that may create some unpleasant results. (We'll discuss this in chapter seven.) It's not forbearance to suppress an offense you can't readily release, or to prefer the pain of being sinned against to what you imagine would be the greater pain of discussing it, or to let a pattern of sin in your spouse go completely unaddressed.

Forbearance applies to specific instances of sin. It involves a clear-eyed realization that we may have been sinned against, and then a bold-hearted, gospel-inspired decision to cover that sin with love. Peter gives us the key to forbearance. "Above all, keep loving one another earnestly, since love covers a multitude of sins" (1 Peter 4:8). Looks like Peter learned the lessons of Luke 6 pretty well.

When we are sinned against, we can cover it—overwrite it, if you will—with the perspective of love. Thus, forbearance includes a commitment to earnestness in our love, actively holding ourselves accountable to keeping the sin covered.

Covering sin with love in effect removes a sin committed from the field of play. This can be extremely helpful during certain seasons. Often in marriages we're working on big issues, a process that can be derailed by small offenses. Sometimes petty sins can be so frequent as to leave us discouraged about making any progress at all. And sometimes one spouse can be in a season of challenge that makes him or her more susceptible to temptation in certain areas. In such instances, forbearance sets aside the smaller issues that could distract or detract from something more important.

For example, at times Kimm and I have the privilege to speak at marriage retreats. While Kimm is greatly honored at these times to address wives on some topic dear to her heart, message preparation is not an area in which she feels gifted. The weeks of preparation leading up to the event, on top of her daily responsibilities, can bring anxious temptations into play. Sometimes this anxiety expresses itself in complaining to me. When we first encountered these seasons, I thought what she needed was perspective, something like, "If Susannah Wesley could run a house with, like, eighty-three kids, and still have a three-hour quiet time, how big was her God?"[5] Pretty slick, huh? Suffice it to say those were never productive conversations.

Thankfully, I've learned it is not only wise but loving to take into account the "heat" in Kimm's life. I need to look for how she's battling it, try to encourage rather than critique, and be willing to let a little of her mud (or well-heated engine oil) splash on me so she can grow in faith through the experience. What a privilege to represent the love of our Savior in forbearing the sins of my spouse for the sake of love. What a reminder of God's forbearance of my sin because of love.

Where do we find forbearance in Luke 6? We need to take a step back to see it. Verse 17 tells us Jesus was speaking to two groups: "a great crowd of his disciples and a great multitude of people." The second group was just like you and me before we became Christians—people who had little real clue they needed a Savior. As Jews, these onlookers were quite confident in their religious standing before God, and simply had no room in their theology to see themselves as enemies of God. They were there for oration and healings, not repentance. Later, many of them would turn against Jesus, calling for his crucifixion. Even his disciples would abandon him, one of them betraying him to death.

There was not one person present that day who had not or would not sin grievously against the Son of God. Even as Jesus spoke of extending mercy to one another, he was extending forbearance to his hearers. The call to mercy came from the merciful Savior himself.

Mercy Defeats Our True Enemy

A number of years ago, I became aware of an ugly assumption that influenced some of my relationships. It went like this: *I shouldn't have to deal with the aggravation of other people's sin.* After all, it was painful, inconvenient, and a real hassle. Plus, I had better and far more important things to do. So when it seemed that people were sinning against me, I reacted in ways that made perfect sense to me, ways that seemed reasonable and even righteous. It felt righteous . . . it was truly *self-righteous*! You can imagine how that played out in our happy home.

Have you ever heard any of these statements slipping past your lips?

"I can't believe you did that!"

"I don't deserve this."

"I've got a right to be angry."

"Why aren't you serious about change?"

Just dripping with mercy, aren't they? Actually, they're leaking the hot oil of self-righteousness. Self-righteousness is a sense of moral superiority that appoints us as prosecutor of other people's sinfulness. We relate to others as if we are incapable of the sins they commit. Self-righteousness wages war against mercy.

It's easy to celebrate the gift of marriage in the midst of a romantic, rosy-eyed honeymoon. But we are fallen folks and that becomes evident in marriage in stark ways. Mercy is most necessary when we encounter the brokenness or frailty of the person we married. It shines bright in particular experiences of life: The moment of sin and the moment of weakness followed by mercy and forgiveness.

How we respond when we think we've been sinned against can reveal self-righteousness. Perhaps the easiest and most common reaction is to assign ourselves as judge, prosecutor, court recorder, and jury. Not surprisingly, these tend to be pretty open-and-shut cases. We begin by mentally assigning a motive to the crime of our defendant-spouse. In a flash of mere moments we usher in the internal jury, present the case, and instantly get back a most unsurprising verdict: "Guilty." Of the actual defendant no questions have been asked, no opportunity for testimony has been given, and no review of the circumstances provided.

Have you dragged your spouse into the Courtroom of Me lately? I have. But here are some questions I've learned to ask myself in the battle with self-righteousness:

• Am I self-confident that I see the supposed "facts" clearly?

- Am I quick to assign motives when I feel I've been wronged?

- Do I find it easy to build a case against someone that makes me seem right and him or her seem wrong?

- Do I ask questions with built-in assumptions I believe will be proven right? Or do I ask impartial questions—the kind that genuinely seek new information regardless of its implications for my preferred outcome?

- Am I overly concerned about who is to blame for something?

- Am I able to dismiss questions like these as irrelevant?

If any of these resonate with you, you might be ensnared in the sin of self-righteousness.

Self-righteousness doesn't just show up when people *sin* against us. It also expresses itself when we encounter the *weaknesses* of others. I don't want to draw too fine a line between sins and weaknesses, because sin in fact has a weakening effect on our character. But the Bible understands weakness—areas of vulnerability or susceptibility to temptation that are different from person to person. We're not all strong in all areas. Some are more susceptible to discouragement than others, or anger, or anxiety. Some struggle with physical weakness more than others. We all have some weakness in some area, or else there would be no need for the power of God to operate in our lives (Romans 8:26).

Weaknesses in our spouse can tempt us—they're inconvenient and frustrating to what we want from our marriage. How do I respond when that particular weakness in my spouse arises *again*? Do I just keep insisting (aloud or silently), "I don't see how that can possibly be a problem for you!" This is a particularly sad expression of self-righteousness. Rather than sympathizing with the weaknesses or limitations of others, we act in condescending and demanding ways. We are finely attuned to the weaknesses of others but slow to see our own.

"For we do not have a high priest who is unable to sympathize with our weaknesses, but one who in every respect has been tempted as we are, yet without sin" (Hebrews 4:15). Scripture assumes we each have weaknesses, and Christ is aware of and extends mercy toward every single one. He can relate to our struggles and calls us to do the same for our spouses.

Would your spouse say you sympathize with weakness? That you extend to him or her the mercy Christ has lavished on you in light of your weaknesses? Or do you sit in judgment?

The good news for self-righteous, judgmental people (all of us from time to time) is that mercy triumphs over judgment (James 2:13). When I grasp the mercy of God expressed to me, it opens my eyes to the bankruptcy of my own righteousness and sends me to the cross for the righteousness of Christ. I can then sympathize with my spouse's weaknesses and rejoice in my own, for they reveal God's strength (2 Corinthians 12:9). As John Stott has said, "God's power operates best in human weakness. Weakness is the arena in which God can most effectively manifest his power."[6]

Mercy Triumphs Over Judgment

There are those who will read this chapter and something in them will cry out, "No! It can't really be like that!" To so many spouses, one more turning of the cheek or one more overlooked sin is just too much. Mercy has been tried and "it hasn't worked." Nothing has changed. In fact, mercy has been trampled on and abused; it just doesn't produce results.

But we must go back and ask, "What is the purpose of mercy?" Do I extend mercy to get a response? Are results the point? Is mercy some spiritual coin with which I purchase my spouse's good behavior?

In Luke 6, Jesus makes it clear that mercy does carry a promise. But it's a promise of reward, not of results (v. 35). Jesus never promises to change our enemies (the extreme case that encompasses all cases). What he has in view for us is a loving relationship with our Father in heaven that will increasingly eclipse any hateful or hurtful actions against us.

Remember Gordon and Emma from the beginning of this chapter? He's the pastor who told his wife on their honeymoon that he had only married her for the sake of his career. It's time to tell the rest of their story.

Gordon's disregard for Emma permeated almost every facet of their marriage. While she continued to live under the same roof, she never experienced life under his care. Seemingly normal on the outside, Gordon's disdain for his marriage created a home ruled by his hypocrisy and indifference to his wife's well-being. His children grew up with a clear sense of the difference in their family and others, but little grasp on the fundamental wrong being done to their mother on a daily basis.

But Emma loved the Savior who was merciful to her and clung to him through the trials and years. Bereft of human love from the man she had wed, she threw herself on the mercy of God. The gospel reminded her that she needed a Savior—and that her principal need was not to be saved from a cruel twist of fate, or the evil of the man who shared her home, but from her own profound sinfulness before God.

Emma understood the mercy and forgiveness of God for her sin, and accepted the Father's call to extend mercy toward her husband. Emma never allowed bitterness to take root in her heart. Instead, she learned how to stand with dignity by entrusting her welfare to Christ.

For four decades, mercy defined her actions, thoughts, and words toward the man whose very purpose in life seemed to be to crush her spirit. Knowing that her response to her husband would testify to her children about the God she served, Emma was resolutely determined to draw on Christ for grace and to honor Christ in her actions.

The marriage ended sadly and painfully after forty years—an apparent ministry call squandered, a financially destitute family shattered by the unrepentant sin of one man. In the years following their divorce, Emma sent Gordon birthday cards and periodic letters, calling the lonely and rebellious man to God. She was tasting the sweet joy of a deep relationship with the Father, and increasingly longed for Gordon to know that for himself.

Somewhere in that time, the mercy of God broke in on Gordon and he responded to the gospel call in saving faith. The children, now adult Christians, lovingly confronted him on his past sins, and for the first time Gordon took responsibility for the destruction of his family. Gordon wrote a letter to Emma confessing his sin against God and against her. Emma was faced with a test that we'll talk about in the next chapter—the test of forgiveness. Can it be that easy? Can mercy cover forty years of wrong? We have Emma's choice preserved in the note she wrote back to her former husband:

It is with mixed emotions that I read your letter. Sad, as I was reminded of many difficult years, but also glad for the work the Spirit of God is doing in your life. Glad to hear you share your failures so frankly and ask for my forgiveness. And glad to hear you share them with your children. Gordon, I forgive you. I forgive you for not loving me as Christ loved the church and for your disregard of our marriage vows. Though I am saddened by many marriage memories, I have released them to the Lord and have guarded my heart from the ravages of bitterness. I rejoice in the mercy of God, that in spite of our failed marriage, our children all serve the Lord faithfully . . . God uses confession and forgiveness to bring healing. I'm trusting God that will be true for both of us.

Both Emma and Gordon have gone on to be with the Savior, who wove restoration into a torn family with the strong threads of mercy. All of their children love the Savior and now see the mysterious purpose of God as they look back. Though Emma and Gordon were never restored as husband and wife, Gordon was laid to rest in old age, no longer alone, surrounded not only by his family but by the friends of his church with whom he had knit his life. Emma's body gave in over time to stroke, but her spirit and story define a work of God that transcends the failure of a marriage and touched many lives.

For Emma, mercy had triumphed over judgment decades before Gordon repented. Mercy triumphed with every prayer cast heavenward, every sin covered in love, every refusal to grow bitter. For Gordon, mercy meant getting what he didn't deserve—the forgiveness of his sins, the love of his family, a home with the Savior, six God-honoring children, Emma's life-long love of Christ. Each of these remarkable outcomes point to the triumphant sweetening effect of mercy—the remarkable mercy Emma received from God and lavished on her family.

Does mercy triumph over judgment? What do you think? I came across these words from Shakespeare which speak a better answer than I could ever give.

> The quality of mercy is not strain'd,
> It droppeth as the gentle rain from heaven
> Upon the place beneath. It is twice blest:
> It blesseth him that gives and him that takes.[7]

Mercy is never strained because it is able to cover all it touches. It sweetens all it touches because it comes from heaven—from the very throne of the merciful Savior. Mercy is a blessing to those who receive and those who give. Take all you can get. And don't forget to pass it on.

Chapter Six

Forgiveness, Full and Free

How to Unite What Sin Has Separated

The agreement was to write off forty billon dollars of debt, an unprecedented move in international relations. The nations represented at the 2005 G8 Summit had decided to cancel the debt of the eighteen highly indebted poor countries in Africa who qualified for debt reduction.[1] It was the largest debt-cancellation in history. The G8's action testified to the member nations' ability to benevolently overlook mere economic interests. Forty billion dollars—that's a lot of zeroes! As the reports confirming this dramatic generosity raced around the globe, one thing became clear: canceling an enormous debt makes an enormous statement.

In the previous chapter we discussed the power of mercy in marriage—how the call to mercy comes from the mercy we've received from God in Christ. In this chapter we look at another aspect of mercy: forgiveness.

In Scripture, the ideas of mercy and forgiveness are so intertwined as to be almost synonymous. But there is an important difference. Mercy can be extended to those who don't recognize it, whereas forgiveness is most often a transaction between parties.[2]

Under the G8 agreement, affluent nations took responsibility for a debt owed by others, while those who owed the debt gladly accepted the forgiveness and moved forward in light of it. As significant as that was, however, chapter 18 of Matthew's gospel addresses the cancellation of a far more significant debt, a cancellation that should make an enormous statement to sinners who say "I do."

The focus of our discussion is a parable prompted by a question from Mr. Can't-think-outside-the-box himself, Simon Peter. The parable begins in Matthew 18:21 where Peter asks, "Lord, how often will my brother sin against me and I forgive him?" Peter is trying to calculate things that don't seem to add up. Jesus has just walked his disciples through a primer for handling the sins of others in the community of faith. Peter wants to get specific—how many times do I need to forgive somebody before I can make them pay what they owe me? Peter was looking to make a deal. "Let's make this a win-win, Lord. We know what forgiveness is worth on the open market. I'll give you seven times right now and we can close this thing."

But Jesus apparently has a different idea of the value of forgiveness. He offers Peter a divine multiplication exercise. How many is seventy times seven? Peter needs more than a calculator. He needs a complete renovation of his understanding of God's love and forgiveness. So Christ introduces Peter to an act of forgiveness that leaves no doubt as to what true forgiveness really costs. Let's join Jesus in the story:

Therefore the kingdom of heaven may be compared to a king who wished to settle accounts with his servants. When he began to settle, one was brought to him who owed him ten thousand talents. And since he could not pay, his master ordered him to be sold, with his wife and children and all that he had, and payment to be made. So the servant fell on his knees, imploring him, "Have patience with me, and I will pay you everything." And out of pity for him, the master of that servant released him and forgave him the debt. But when that same servant went out, he found one of his fellow servants who owed him a hundred denarii, and seizing him, he began to choke him, saying, "Pay what you owe." So his fellow servant fell down and pleaded with him, "Have patience with me, and I will pay you." He refused and went and put him in prison until he should pay the debt. When his fellow servants saw what had taken place, they were greatly distressed, and they went and reported to their master all that had taken place. Then his master summoned him and said to him, "You wicked servant! I forgave you all that debt because you pleaded with me. And should not you have had mercy on your fellow servant, as I had mercy on you?" And in anger his master delivered him to the jailers, until he should pay all his debt. So also my heavenly Father will do to every one of you, if you do not forgive your brother from your heart.

(Matthew 18:23–35)

To help Peter (and all of us) understand, the Lord tells the parable of a king who forgives a debt of 10,000 talents, a number beyond the comprehension of his hearers. The forgiven debtor then encounters a fellow debtor who owes him 100 denarii, about 4 months of work for a day laborer—a pretty serious chunk-of-change—but microscopic compared to what he was forgiven. When the fellow debtor is unable to pay, the forgiven debtor throws him into prison. The king finds out what has happened "And in anger his master delivered him to the jailers, until he should pay all his debt." In order to avoid any confusion, the Lord summarizes the parable in verse 35. "So also my heavenly Father will do to every one of you." In that moment, the Lord wasn't looking only at Peter or only at his disciples. He was scanning us all, your marriages and mine, saying precisely that if we refuse to forgive one another, "So also my heavenly Father will do to every one of you."

In case this throws you—if it seems to suggest that God is unmerciful to his own children—let me emphasize the driving truth of this parable. Extending true forgiveness is clear and persuasive evidence that we have been forgiven by God. The bottom line is that *forgiven sinners forgive sin.*

In the previous chapter we discussed forbearance, the grace to overlook offenses against us for the sake of Christ. Forbearance comes into play when we are truly able to cover a perceived offense with God's love, not retaining the smallest resentment. This chapter covers a different subject—sin that cannot be overlooked, but must be dealt with for the sake of Christ. We're going to talk about the forgiveness that is required when sin is acknowledged and confessed. And we're going to seek to define forgiveness in a biblical way, perhaps in a way you've never understood or practiced it.

In my experience as a pastor, there may be no more misapplied or under-applied means of grace in marriage than forgiveness. But when in marriage forgiveness is expressed according to truth, there may be no greater agent for change and hope. To help us keep our discussion of forgiveness grounded in the real world, let me introduce a true-life parable, the story of my friends Jeremy and Cindy.

A Marriage in Bankruptcy

You probably know Jeremy and Cindy. You've seen them around, or at least someone like them. They're the couple who have it all together—sharp, attractive, gifted—great role models in the church. But sometimes having it all together on the outside simply masks the chaos within, and this marriage was certainly in chaos.

As ambitious "Type A" personalities, both of them were getting a lot done in life. They fell in love and seemed destined to be together. After the gorgeous wedding they settled into an upper-middle-class life, but it didn't take long to realize that this was not what either had envisioned.

A two-career couple, each assumed they would navigate through this marriage thing as a team. Instead, a subtle competition developed between them. Pride and selfishness increasingly drove their personal lives. As their personal ambitions pulled in different directions, gaps quickly opened in the weak foundation of their marriage. In all the busyness of life, neither one could see the fissures growing.

Jeremy began to wander, first with his thoughts, then increasingly and more boldly with his actions, until he had given himself fully to an adulterous relationship. As he describes it:

Pride fueled my actions and thoughts. My opinions were the only correct ones and I had a "right" to have all my needs met. Whenever Cindy pointed out areas where she felt I could grow, I quickly countered with all the great things she was overlooking and how "lucky" she was to be married to me. To my humiliation and shame, when we argued I would often say things like "any other woman would love to be married to me." Instead of dealing humbly with the growing problems, I chose to run from my God-given responsibilities and vows, and pursued a relationship with another woman.

This running led to a gradual hardening of my heart and manifested itself in an arrogant attempt to see how close I could get to the flame and not get burnt. As I invested my thoughts and time in this ungodly relationship, I had decreasing interest at home in Cindy. The superficial shell of religion was no match for the deceit and power of lust. What began as a worldly attraction eventually spiraled into adultery. During

101

the months leading up to my physical adultery, I experienced uncommon sleeplessness and anxiety. It was as if I was running down a train track toward an unseen but audible oncoming train. I knew the right thing to do would be to jump off the track but I continued running faster, somehow drawn in by the "excitement" of the feelings. Rejecting God's patience as he gave me months of opportunity to turn from my sin, I chose to run headlong into the abyss.

(If I can make a plea—husbands and wives, should you find yourself en route to the abyss of infidelity, whether with a person or with pornography in any of its manifestations, please repent of your sin and seek the help of a person you trust. Read this story as a warning and a plea from the God who loves you and is seeking to rescue you from that sin. And to the men especially—guys, please don't place yourself over Jeremy, but rather identify with him. We are all more like him than we may imagine.)

We'll be following the testimony of Jeremy and Cindy throughout this chapter. But let's put it on hold for now and learn some more about how forgiveness works, especially in marriage.

Forgiveness Reckons with the Holy God

When we use human standards of evaluation, we can begin to think our "run-of-the-mill" sins against our spouse (indifference, laziness, or unkind speech, for example) are on the level of a "100-denarii sin." And we could easily look at Jeremy's sin as a "10,000-talent sin." This kind of thinking can lead us to assume that if our sin isn't as bad as someone else's (my spouse's, for example), my problem with God can't be as bad, either. But to let my thoughts go there is to miss completely not only the lessons of the Matthew 18 parable but the heart of the gospel as well.

Certainly, many wives and husbands are sinned against horribly. Some who read these words suffer under the cloud of awful abuses committed against them, whether physical or emotional, and spouses who no longer seem to care. Yet, as we saw in chapter two, we do not truly grasp the good news of Jesus Christ in the gospel until we see that our sin against a holy God is a far greater injustice than anything that could be done to us.

Our loving Father cares deeply about the severity of any sins committed against you. In his perfect holiness and omniscience he overlooks not a single sin. But in that same holiness and omniscience he also sees your every sin, no matter how great, no matter how small, and regardless of the circumstances which bring it to light.

This is to say that in the eyes of our compassionate and loving God, sin is sin, guilt is guilt, and all sin is against his limitless holiness. My petty indifference to my wife is sufficient to warrant the full wrath of a holy God and required the blood of my Savior to take it away.

Yes, some sins that spouses commit against one another can biblically and rationally be seen as larger, and some as smaller. But Jesus was intentional to make the forgiving voice in this drama a character rich beyond our wildest imagination and magnanimous with dazzling grace. This master (representing God) was inconceivably benevolent toward the ungrateful servant (representing us) who by his behavior demonstrated that he had completely missed the significance of what had been done for him.

You see, the *status of the one sinned against is key*, and the fact that all sin is against God locates every one of us in the 10,000-talent camp—a central point of this parable. In *The Valley of Vision*, one of the Puritans prayed, "Let me never forget that the heinousness of sin lies not so much in the nature of the sin committed, as in the greatness of the Person sinned against."[3] The "size" of a sin is not ultimately determined by the sin itself, but by the one who is sinned against. Sin is infinitely wicked because it rejects the one who is infinitely holy and good. The more we recognize the perfection of God's holiness, the more obvious this truth becomes.

For the sake of our marriages we must see ourselves in the shoes of the 10,000-talent debtor. The appreciation of a massive debt forgiven (our sin against a holy God) forms the base and starting point for our forgiveness of one another's much smaller (by comparison) offenses. Without understanding the depth of our sin against God and the riches of his forgiveness toward us, we will never be able to forgive others.

So as we continue to relate to Jeremy and Cindy, let's just own up to that 10,000-talent debt. We all need someone to stand between us and the justified wrath of God. We all need the Savior. Second Corinthians 5 speaks of our need this way, "He made him to be sin, who knew no sin, so that in him we might become the righteousness of God." Jesus paid our debt and gave us his perfect standing before his holy Father.

In commenting on this parable, Puritan Matthew Henry wrote, "If that is the measure of the forgiveness the disciple has received, any limitation on the forgiveness he shows to his brother is unthinkable."[4] That's why this parable ends with such a somber warning. God will not have his holy forgiveness mocked.

As we are about to see, it was Jeremy's confrontation with the holy God that ultimately led him to confess his adultery to his wife.

> I believe God used the unbridled nature of my sin, which I could not blame on anyone, and its devastating effect on Cindy, to bring me to my senses and confess my need for the Savior. I abandoned all previous religious confidence and threw myself on God's mercy. As much as I desired Cindy's forgiveness and the restoration of our marriage, I knew my greatest need was for God's forgiveness. My heartfelt confession occurred one lonely night. "God, even if Cindy chooses to pursue divorce

(which I knew she had every biblical right to do) I know I have no right to this marriage. All I've ever deserved was your wrath. Forgive me for my adultery in heart and action against you and her, based only on your Son's shed blood. I accept him and his work, and whatever discipline you require to change my heart."

There arose from the ashes of my confession the first genuine love for God that I ever knew. I desired to be the husband and father God had called me to be. I had proven myself both unworthy of these titles and incapable of fulfilling them. I was, for the first time in my life, facing my weakness and insufficiency for a task. All my life, I believed I could do anything if I just applied myself. Now, I knew that any fruit in my life had to be a work of God and I was simply a recipient of his grace and gifts. I couldn't erase the pain of the past or instill hope for the future. I couldn't create in our home a peace that passes understanding. I couldn't change Cindy's heart to forgive or love me. Only a God with the power to save a sinner like me could restore a marriage as damaged as ours.

The road back for Jeremy began on his knees at the foot of the cross. He was a weak and broken man. Just what his marriage needed.

Forgiveness is Costly

What about Cindy? How did Jeremy's adultery affect her?

When I became aware of my husband's adultery, our fast-paced life seemed to screech to a halt. A darkness and loneliness which I'd never experienced before engulfed me. Every experience and every situation was tainted with an overwhelming sorrow and darkness—almost as if someone had died. I turned to God and cried out desperately for help day and night, but the pain was so intense. Fear of the future, the sting of betrayal, and the question, "Why did God allow this to happen?" swirled around me constantly. My emotions would fluctuate severely between feelings of great sadness, intense anger, jealousy, fear, and even civility, which in hindsight, I believe, was rooted in a self-protecting desire not to see my marriage fail. I began to question God's character, charging him as harsh, unfaithful, and even cruel. I would give full vent to my thoughts in angry outbursts and bouts of crying. I would then go deep into condemnation and depression. Even my dreams were frightening—awakening me at night. As time progressed, I withdrew a lot and spent a great deal of time alone.

I know there are some reading this book who taste Cindy's words as your own. Reality, cold and hard, whether from a spouse's infidelity or some other deeply painful sin against you, has struck home. Now you find yourself faced with a situation you wish would just go away, although you know it won't. So you are faced with the choice of whether or not to forgive your spouse. It's a choice complicated by something all Christians come to learn.

Forgiveness is costly, and sometimes it costs more than we think we can give.

It's as though forgiveness flows between us through a pipe having three valves. All three must be open for forgiveness to move from one person to another. The first valve, controlled by the one who sinned, is repentance and a request for forgiveness. You see how Jeremy began to turn that first valve. He saw his sin as first and foremost against God, and renounced any claim to his own righteousness. He expressed his repentance—a determined commitment to turn from his sin to God's ways—by accepting the full consequences of his actions and by desiring to please God no matter what the cost. Out of this sorrow for his sin and resolve to live out repentance, he humbly asked forgiveness from Cindy with no demand on her response. True forgiveness is best triggered by the offender turning his or her valve first.

The other two valves are controlled by the one sinned against, and these valves can be every bit as difficult to turn as the first.

Valve two is a mercy valve. It releases the person who sinned from the liability of suffering punishment for that sin. To open this valve, the one sinned against must lay down the temptation to say along with the unforgiving servant, "Pay what you owe!" It shuts off the flow of bitterness by opening the flow of love. Remember Emma's response to Gordon's confession in our last chapter. How easy would it have been for Emma to open the floodgates of accusation from years of heartlessness? Instead Emma "covered over" years of sin against her with grace-empowered mercy—a mercy that has made all the difference in her family ever since.

Opening the third valve requires the willingness of the one sinned against to absorb the cost of the sin. You received emotional pain over what she did. Will the pain end with you or will you return it? You endured a blow to your trust because of what he's done over a period of time. Will your heart attempt to force him to pay what he owes? Or will you follow the footsteps of the master and demonstrate a willingness to absorb the cost?

A natural response to our spouse's sin is pure Matthew 18:28—pay what you owe me, and do it now. Our emotional reaction is not always a spiritual response, even if it "feels right." We fear God's methods don't work. The biblical response—the idea of completely, forthrightly, and permanently forgiving a spouse and releasing him or her from all liability—can seem not only impossibly difficult but less than fully just.

In the end, the most common outcome is some wishy-washy middle ground—neither the sinful tantrum of demanding satisfaction or the godly extension of true forgiveness. It may be the inch-deep, "Oh, it's okay," that tries to pretend nothing ever happened. Perhaps it's the quick, "Of course, I forgive you" (while implying "as long as you never do anything like that again!"). Of course, we may instead simply refuse to forgive, holding our spouse's sin over the head like an old arrest warrant that could be prosecuted at any moment—what the Bible calls bitterness.

But true forgiveness sees another's sin for the evil that it is, addresses it, then absorbs the cost of that sin by the power of God's abundant grace. Such forgiveness sets the sinner free; the account of the sin is closed, cancelled, blotted out, just as we see in Matthew 18. Ken Sande says:

> Forgiveness can be a costly activity. When you cancel a debt, it does not just simply disappear. Instead, you absorb a liability that someone else deserves to pay. Similarly, forgiveness requires that you absorb certain effects of another person's sins and you release that person from liability to punishment. This is precisely what Christ accomplished on Calvary.[5]

So there it is. There is nothing in us that would naturally choose the way of full, biblical forgiveness. It's just too hard, and adding to the challenge is the fact that the extension of true forgiveness can never guarantee we won't be wronged again. So why even consider it? Because forgiveness, full and free, is precisely what has been accomplished for us on Calvary. And the one who has been forgiven is now able to forgive others. Forgiven sinners forgive sin.

It is this truth that ultimately made the difference for Cindy in responding to Jeremy's confession. This may shock you, but in order to forgive Jeremy for his sin, Cindy had to first get a fresh look at her own sin.

> I knew what God's Word said about forgiveness—that I could and should freely forgive in light of Christ's great mercy for me on the cross. Yet, I was not able to see my own sin as clearly, and that became a stumbling block for me to extend forgiveness to Jeremy. It was a process that took time, and

it seemed unbearably slow. At times, I did not think I would make it. Many times I wanted to give up and leave the marriage—I was shortsighted and wanted to stop the pain then and there (which I thought leaving would accomplish), but I was not carefully considering the long-term consequences. By God's grace alone, I did not take that path. I would slip into bitterness often, repent, and start over numerous times. But the more I heard the gospel preached, the more I was able to understand it and apply it to myself.

Over time, I began to see my own sinfulness and God's grace and mercy for my sins. It was very hard to look at my own contribution to the breakdown of our marriage. I wanted to just focus on his part and leave the blame there, but God opened my eyes and helped me to see that, even as a victim of my husband's sin I could not claim innocence in my marriage, and certainly not before a holy God. The gospel gave me power to forgive my husband. Christ had died for both our sins, dying in our place and drinking the full cup of God's wrath we both deserved for our sins. Through the revelation of that truth, I was humbled and disarmed—we were more alike than different. From this standing place, forgiveness flowed.

How that looked practically, though, was not always smooth. There were days when God would break in and reveal the gospel and himself to me in incredible ways. I would experience hope and joy and feel forgiving. Then there were the mundane times—the day-in and day-out, when I did not feel anything, yet God taught me to rely not on my feelings but on his grace to me on the cross. This, I would come to realize, was a fundamental change in my character that God desired to do in me—to become gospel-centered and live my life out of that center.

It was perhaps one of the most difficult things Cindy had ever done. But she was able to genuinely forgive Jeremy when she understood that all sin is against God, and that the gospel of Christ's forgiveness encompasses her sin as well as his.

Forgiveness Releases the Old to Build the New

As we have seen, Jesus' parable in Matthew 18 ends with a sober warning: those who don't forgive won't be forgiven. Jesus wanted Peter to see that his conditional approach to forgiveness looked nothing like the forgiveness in the kingdom that Christ was bringing into the world. And we, like Peter, need to see that forgiveness is not the stuff of the extraordinary saint. Forgiveness is at the heart of the gospel and therefore is to be a defining characteristic of every believer.

To practice forgiveness to full effect, there is one last thing we need to understand about it: how to fully align our motivation for extending forgiveness to God's purpose for forgiveness.

The goal of God's amazing, audacious forgiveness is evident in the context Jesus establishes for the parable of the unforgiving servant. Just before this parable, in Matthew 18:15–19, Jesus discusses how to deal with unrepentant sin in a local-church setting. He closes that discussion with an affirmation of his kingdom reign: "For where two or three are gathered in my name, there am I among them" (Matthew 18:20). (That's when Peter jumps in to ask how many times he is required to forgive someone.)

Thus, the focus of Matthew 18:21–35, as well as the preceding seven verses, is how sinners are to relate to each other in God's kingdom. The underlying assumption is that while sin can be assumed "wherever two or three are gathered," it is never meant to divide. Here, the gut-level reality of living after the Fall crosses with forgiveness, providing hope for even the most distressed marriages.

So we see that forgiveness must be exercised out of more than simply a desire to avoid God's disapproval or to drive away the emotional pain caused by sins against us. Forgiveness was God's idea, was modeled perfectly in Christ, and is commanded in Scripture. Having forgiven us, God does not intend us to remain merely forgiven loiterers in God's kingdom. We are called to pursue true biblical forgiveness, that

God's people might truly be one, and one to a unique and extraordinary extent in marriage.

The gospel, let us remember, has created something astounding—relationships among sinners where the King's rule is experienced and expressed! Do you see your marriage that way? Do you see it as two sinners experiencing and expressing the rule of Christ in the most significant human relationship he has created? When sinners say "I do," they acknowledge the Son of God's presence and Lordship in the endeavor of marriage.

Are you reeling from the grievous sin of your spouse? If he or she came to you with sincere, contrite confession, would you be prepared to forgive? Remember, forgiven sinners forgive sin. Let Cindy inspire you from her experience.

As time passed, God was changing both of us. I could see genuine changes in my husband, but I was very reticent to trust him again. But gradually restoration did occur. I began to look forward to being with him and that anticipation has only increased over the years—and continues! God was restoring us, and as we followed him and delighted in him, our individual relationships with the Lord spilled over to one another. There seemed to be an unending supply of grace, and hope was rekindled in my heart—along with much joy. God has brought me to the place where I can honestly say that I love my husband with all my heart and desire to follow him in everything as he follows God—a miracle of grace.

One other area that really changed for me was how I began to view God's character. I began to see him as good, faithful, and kind. This came mostly, I believe, from hearing the gospel preached and knowing his forgiveness for me, but also from seeing it lived out in my husband, in our family, and in others around me. This led to great hope and vision which I know contributed to the restoration of our marriage. Since then God has continued to show me his great love through the cross. I have learned that I can't exhaust my understanding of the gospel, so I feel beckoned to continue to pursue daily a further understanding of his grace for me.

I stand amazed at the quiet miracle we have experienced—and it was all possible because of his victory over my sin on Calvary. He has shown me that my life is not about me, but rather it's about him, and that in turn is good for me. His ways are not mine, but they are good and trustworthy. And the riches of the gospel, the pearl of great price, is mine in Christ—which will be a firm foundation for me all the way home.

If forgiveness has been lacking in your marriage, perhaps God has a quiet miracle in store for you and your spouse, too.

Or could it be that, like Jeremy in earlier days, there is some ongoing guilt or habit of sin against your spouse for which you have not confessed and repented? If so, pursue the grace that I believe God wants to make available to you through what you have been reading here. What you need is the wisdom to humble yourself, discarding all explanations, justifications, and defenses under the penetrating gaze of the God who knows all. Are you ready to own your sin against God and others through confession and repentance? Let's hear from Jeremy one last time:

The epilogue to our story is one of God's faithfulness to an unfaithful sinner. The depth of my sin stands in stark contrast to the inexhaustible glory of God's grace. From this tragedy, I know in a unique way that no one is ever too far removed from the grace of God.

It took years for God to restore our marriage. Though the memory of our dark years will never be erased, there is an undeniable cleansing of the past. When Scripture says that the Lord will restore the years that the locusts have eaten, I feel as if that passage was written with us in mind. I love Cindy more every year and she has proven countless times her unconditional forgiveness of me. I know that this is only possible because of the shed blood of our Savior. He has given me a righteousness not my own which overwhelms all my sin. It is as if we have lived two separate marriages—and in reality we have. I wish so many things were different. I wish that I had never committed adultery and caused Cindy such pain. I wish that I could tell my children that I had been faithful to my wife from the day we were married. However, because of my sin, these are only wishes. And ultimately, my wishes pale in comparison to God's plan. I will likely never know in this lifetime why God chose to use my sin to get us to where we are now. However, we are beyond asking those questions because they are eclipsed by the glory of God's forgiveness and blessing. By God's grace we no longer look back with regret but rather forward with anticipation to what he has called us to.

The memories remain, yet they no longer influence our lives. Each year, our marriage is sweeter and more satisfying than the one before. By fixing our eyes on the Savior, he has done far more abundantly that all we could ask or think. How amazing is that!

Forgiveness and repentance is the powerful tool that repairs the damage done to sin-torn marriage relationships. And where forgiveness is employed, and repentance is lived out, it transforms. Forgiveness humbly sought, and humbly given, profoundly expresses the glory of God. Why? Because forgiveness is at the heart of the gospel—the true demonstration of God's love for those who deserved his wrath. As John Newton said so well, "The unchangeableness of the Lord's love, and the riches of his mercy, are likewise more illustrated by the multiplied pardons he bestows upon his people, than if they needed no forgiveness at all."[6]

We have been forgiven the greatest debt. Let's learn how to forgive the debtor we married. It's the way forward when sinners say "I do."

Chapter Seven

The Surgeon, the Scalpel, and the Spouse in Sin

Spiritual Surgery for Sinners

*I*t happened, late one afternoon . . ." So begins the account in the book of 2 Samuel. It is the story of a most despicable series of acts—adultery, deception, and murder, made all the more shocking because it was committed by the greatest and most honorable king in the entire history of Israel.

David, the man after God's own heart (1 Samuel 13:14), took extraordinary risks first to indulge and then to disguise his adultery with Bathsheba. Upon learning that she was pregnant by him, David brought her husband home from war in an effort to publicly justify the pregnancy. When that failed, David perverted his authority to the extreme by arranging for the man to be killed in battle. To tie up the package, David then made Bathsheba one of his wives.

A year passed, Bathsheba's child was an infant, and judgment for David's sin was nowhere to be seen. Perhaps he thought he had hidden his wickedness, fooling nearly everyone. Maybe even God. Problem over—close call. Shielded by the trappings of power, he could feel safe, protected, and raised above the mere laws of men by his own cunning, power, and exalted position.

But David and all he cherished were on a collision course with God's justice. Ascending the palace steps was his old friend, the prophet Nathan. And this wasn't a social call. It was a rescue mission.

Nathan stood before a man he loved but hardly recognized, a king deceived and drifting perilously toward destruction. The prophet took no joy in the sharp words forming in his mind. He had no way to predict how David would respond to his rebuke. But when someone close to you is running from the truth, love demands that you speak. Sometimes love must risk peace for the sake of truth. David was about to be loved in one of the hardest possible ways. And he didn't even have to leave the house.

Nathan told David the story of a rich man who had taken a poor man's only sheep to feed some guests. Infuriated by this injustice, David announced that such a man deserved to die. Nathan's timeless reproof was, "You are the man."

The Need for a Nathan

There are two amazing dynamics at work in this historical snapshot. First, God pursues sinners. God's love is relentless. Even when we are blinded by sin, he refuses to let go. God pursued David with a tireless love.

Second, God uses sinners to pursue sinners. Nathan, like David, was a man prone to the same temptations and failures as David. But God had given Nathan a ministry in that moment. He was a sinner called to help another sinner become reconciled to God.

Nathan's role in David's restoration foreshadows something very significant about the gospel. Jesus, God's Son, would later come to confront our sin. Through his sacrifice on the cross, he has put our sin away and reconciled us to God (Romans 5:10). But also, as we have been learning, those granted a Savior are called to imitate their Savior. So far in this book we have begun to learn how to imitate Christ in mercy and forgiveness. Here, we will begin to learn about biblical confrontation and reproof for the purpose of reconciliation.

Paul says in 2 Corinthians 5 that we have been given the ministry of reconciliation. It is reconciliation between a sinner and God, and between a sinner and the one(s) sinned against. This is a ministry not only to God's enemies for their salvation, but—our focus in this chapter—to God's sin-struggling children for their ongoing growth and relationship to him. To whomever we may be ministering reconciliation, God literally makes his appeals through us (1 Corinthians 5:17–21).

In addition, James informs us that we are to be peacemakers for the sake of righteousness (James 3:18). That is, we must be willing to use relational ties to intervene and help our brothers and sisters walk in a manner worthy of their calling. Charles Spurgeon drives this point home. "Our love ought to follow the love of God in one point, namely, in always seeking to produce reconciliation. It was to this end that God sent his Son."[1]

Aren't you glad Nathan had enough courage to deliver truth to a king in the grip of "sin and spin"? We may not undermine kingdoms by our sin, but the effect of unrepentant sin harms ourselves, families, relationships, churches, businesses, ministries, and careers in often devastating ways. Over time, even "moral misdemeanors" and sins that may seem petty compared to David's can do deep damage. We all need a Nathan. We all need someone who can discern a slow drift or a rapid freefall from God, look us in the eye, and say, "You are the one."

It's inevitable. In navigating through a fallen world with a sinful heart, from time to time your spouse will experience a pattern of sin that extinguishes joy and saps the soul, revealing dangerous corrosion in one's character or relationship with God. Perhaps, just like David, your spouse will even be locked in denial and doing everything possible to hide the truth. Such sin cannot, must not, go unaddressed.

Look around. Who can play the Nathan role for your spouse? Who will take on the ministry of reconciliation? This needs to be someone appointed by God, close enough to see, and humble enough to be concerned more about God's righteousness than about people's opinions. There's really only one likely candidate: You.

What will you do in those times when truth is absolutely necessary? What will you do when your spouse needs a Nathan?

Beyond Self-Examination

To answer this, let's return to the discussion of Matthew 7 we began in chapter four. It's the speck and the log again. We have already seen in the passage that when it comes to confrontation the first step is self-examination and self-suspicion, taking the log out of our own eye. But of course, that's just the beginning.

> Or how can you say to your brother, "Let me take the speck out of your eye," when there is the log in your own eye? You hypocrite, first take the log out of your own eye, *and then you will see clearly to take the speck out of your brother's eye* (Matthew 7:3–5, emphasis added).

118

Seems obvious now, doesn't it? This passage does not stop at log-removal. Clearing the timber is an essential means to a greater end.

The passage above gives two reasons why we must begin with our own logs. First, dealing with our own sin helps us to "see clearly" (v. 5). Removing my sin grants me the perspective and clarity that comes with humility. It improves my discernment and clears away much of the debris obstructing my view. We'll never be able to see 20/20 in this life, but cutting away my own log lets me see through the lens of compassion and care rather than the searing eyes of judgment and self-righteousness.

Second, a little lumber work prepares me for the Savior's ultimate goal. Gaining perspective has a purpose: ministry to others, in this case my spouse. Self-examination *alone* cannot produce a sweet marriage, but *only* self-examination can provide the humble clarity of sight I need to serve my spouse. My own logging efforts position me for speck-removal.

The Work of Grace and Truth

Maurice hasn't committed murder or adultery. He hasn't taken great pains to cover up dark deeds. Yet Maurice needs a Nathan.

His company is being downsized, his position is "under review," and Maurice is fretting. The future is uncertain and jobs in his field are slim pickings. Around the house, his countenance reveals his anxiety. Once-vibrant dinner conversations have been replaced by long sighs and longer silences. When his wife asks why, Maurice says he just needs room to think. Like David, he doesn't see his spiritual slide. But Maurice is slipping, gradually yet steadily, into a world of worry, a captivating, mind-numbing exercise of rolling over each possibility to consider all angles and outcomes, as if analyzing his circumstances and controlling them are the same thing.

Maurice talks about faith and trusting God, but his comments seem thin and obligatory, a denial of the true battle within. Sleepless nights tell the real story. Awake and staring into darkness, Maurice's imagination runs wild—there he is, unemployed, the house foreclosed, his family begging in the streets. A bead of sweat forms on his brow. Maurice lies alone in the dark, like a man with no God.

Maurice needs understanding from a loving wife who sympathizes with his trial. She must pray for him and encourage him in his efforts to lead and provide for his family. But he also needs something else from her. He needs her to be a Nathan. Someone who knows him and loves him enough to carefully direct truth to his God-denying worry. Someone within the home who can both stand on God's promises and speak them with loving conviction.

Interesting, isn't it, how sinners who say "I do" exist in an ironic biblical tension? We are called to be merciful and withhold judgment. But we are also called to challenge one another—to correct, exhort, and speak truth to the one we love (Hebrews 3:12–13). This can seem like a paradox, even an apparent contradiction in our call. But it's not. On the contrary, God has set us in our marriage, at this time, with this person so that we can perform an extraordinary task of ministry. We can fulfill the call of reconciliation—turning a wandering believer back to the God who saves. We can love by bringing truth in gracious ways; applying grace through speaking the truth. When we do this ministry, we not only fulfill the role of Nathan, we represent our Lord Jesus Christ, who came and dwelt among us, full of grace and truth (John 1:14).

Okay, so how exactly do we do this work of grace and truth?

The Surgeon and the Saint In Sin

Matthew Henry once said, "The three qualifications of a good surgeon are requisite in a reprover: He should have an eagle's eye, a lion's heart, and a lady's hand; in short, he should be endued with wisdom, courage, and meekness."[2]

This great Puritan had struck upon a wonderful metaphor. Reproof—the means by which a Nathan reaches into the soul of one trapped in sin to bring the ministry of reconciliation—is a lot like surgery. Both require care, wisdom, and precision, as well as a delicate and determined hand.

Of course, when Matthew Henry wrote those words some three hundred years ago, about the only thing surgery had in common with surgery today was the goal of making people well by rearranging their innards. There were no micro-surgical techniques, no arthroscopy, no anesthesia, no sterilization, no antibiotics, no germ theory. It was a crude and gruesome business. Nevertheless, those Puritan-era docs dedicated themselves to the task of physical care with all they could bring to the table. They knew they actually understood very little, yet they were deeply committed to trying to help and to learn all they could, that they might help even more.

When it comes to soul-surgery, we're a lot like those physicians of Puritan times. We scarcely understand ourselves, so how can we understand someone else? The one thing we do know is that we don't even know what we don't know! The skills we possess seem so inadequate, we wonder if it wouldn't be less traumatic to the "patient" to do nothing at all.

All the same, we are called to this specialized surgical task, appointed by God to exercise all our abilities, however meager, yet to rely on him for the outcome. The essential instruments in this work have never changed: Wisdom, courage, and meekness.

A Good Surgeon Displays Wisdom

Here's a brief lesson, drawn from the Harvey Surgical Records, in how not to bring correction.

It was a really nice restaurant—the kind where a guy in a tuxedo seats you and inquires politely about your preference in bottled water. There was candlelight, coat-checking (no numbers—they just remember your name), original art on the walls, and classical music drifting through the rooms. A quick look at the menu revealed we would pay dearly for the ambience (at least the prices were listed!). But that didn't matter. Everything was perfect. This would be a memorable date night.

And it was indeed memorable. Just not for the reasons I had hoped.

If I could choose my own superpower, it would be the ability to suck back stupid statements the instant they escape my lips. I could have used it that night when I offered my wife a few observations that I had been holding for "just the right time." Turns out that evening was not the right time. Not even close. Thanks to me, what we experienced that night was just a very expensive conflict. Nothing ruins a good dinner like a bad argument.

A wise surgeon, you see, chooses the right time. But soul surgery and fine restaurants don't go together. At least, not for Kimm and me. In choosing that evening to begin the delicate work of surgery, I was displaying a marked absence of wisdom.

"The beginning of wisdom is this: get wisdom, and whatever you get, get insight" (Proverbs 4:7). That's clear enough, but what *is* wisdom? As we saw in chapter four, wisdom begins with the fear of the Lord—living practically in view of God's glory. Or, as J. I. Packer has written, "Not till we have become humble and teachable, standing in awe of God's holiness and sovereignty, acknowledging our own littleness, distrusting our own thoughts, and willing to have our minds turned upside down, can divine wisdom become ours."[3]

Nathan's approach to David is biblical wisdom on display. Nathan chose the right time and then did the reaching out, going to the palace to see his old friend, the king. He chose a wise method, the story of the stolen lamb, to carefully entice David to look at himself. And he was very clear about the nature of the sin and who bore the blame. In response, David could have easily made life miserable for Nathan, but Nathan took the risk anyway. Why? Because Nathan feared God more than he feared David. Nathan was a wise man, concerned for the interests of God above all else.

To become truly wise in confronting sin, here are a couple of crucial surgical techniques to employ.

Patients Should Know They Need Help

Imagine a surgeon approaching strangers on a busy street and offering his services, "Excuse me, ma'am, anything I can cut out of you today?" This approach is more likely to attract law enforcement than it is business. We all know that good surgeons don't trawl for patients. They operate on those who want and need their services.

Marriages grow sour when spouses engage in surgery casually, carelessly, or without the informed consent of the patient. But marriage becomes sweet when spouses, recognizing that each one will probably need corrective surgery from time to time, give one another permission to wield the scalpel as needed.

An excellent and humble way to demonstrate your ongoing willingness to come under the biblical knife is to pursue correction regularly. This tells your spouse that if you need surgery, you want surgery. My friend Mark often asks me if I have any thoughts or observations about his character or behavior. In this regard he's a "model patient," and I want to import his example into my marriage. It's important to me that Kimm is aware that I *want* correction, not that I will merely tolerate it. When I pursue correction it tells her she is welcome to operate, because I know I need the help.

Never Cut Blindly

If you or someone close to you has had surgery recently, you're probably aware of the extensive medical analysis that takes place before the patient gets anywhere near the operating room. Batteries of tests are run, consultations held, pre-op meds administered. The cynic may say this is to avoid lawsuits, but there is wisdom at work: the better the preparation, the better the outcome is likely to be. This applies to the surgery of reproof as well. The better prepared we are to speak truth, the more likely that truth will be heard and taken to heart. The fine-dining experience I had hoped to enjoy with Kimm became a poor dining experience for one simple reason. I cut blindly.

Here are some diagnostic pre-op questions to help you operate wisely when it's time to give surgical reproof.

- *Have I prayed for God's wisdom and acknowledged my need for his help in serving my spouse?* Prayer is not just some formality we walk through before wheeling our spouse into the spiritual operating room. It should be a heartfelt expression of our dependence upon God. In prayer we are reminded of our surgical limitations—we can operate, but we cannot heal; we can speak, but we cannot convict concerning sin. Only God can do that (John 16:8). Prayer brings the fear of the Lord to the forefront of our minds, and this is the beginning of wisdom. If we connect with God before we move toward sinners, it becomes far easier to draw them back to him.

- *Are my observations based upon patterns of behavior or merely a single incident?* Beware of seizing a single illustration—what I like to call *sola illustrate*—to press home some significant concern for your spouse's soul. If you tend to rush into spiritual appendectomies at the first sign of a tummy-ache-size sin, it probably means your pre-op skills are weak. How are you doing on praying for your spouse, forbearing with your spouse, and loving your spouse?

- *Am I content to address one area of concern, even if I'm aware of several?* Don't you wish change was as efficient as a surgical procedure? (Yes, the surgery analogy is far from perfect.) Just imagine: chronic anger today, operation tomorrow morning, a couple of days watching the tube during recovery, and the anger is gone with maybe a little scar to show for the trouble! But life is different. Transformation takes place in the midst of daily hustle and bustle. The kids still need to be fed and the bills paid while we struggle through our brokenness. It can be discouragingly hard to focus on more than one area of growth at a time. A good surgeon keeps that in mind.

- *Am I committed to making incisions no larger than absolutely necessary?* When trying to bring a spouse to a point of godly conviction over sin, too often we overwhelm him or her with a great volume of information or a litany of examples. We may think this is the quickest way to attain the goal, but often the force of our communication propels our spouse right past conviction and into the septic infection of condemnation. When it comes to change, we often want a "quick fix," but "God sets about a long slow answering."[4] To be wise in grace is to see that a well-considered word carefully applied is good medicine. This is a soul you're slicing open. Go very slowly. Cut very gently.

- *Am I prepared to humbly offer an observation rather than an assumption or conclusion?* You and I will never have perfect insight into our spouse's heart. To assume we do is to be judgmental, and judging is reserved for God. In his mystery and mercy, God withholds from us definitive insight into another's heart, even for two people who can finish each other's sentences. Thus, the most helpful surgery is often exploratory. Similarly, the most helpful reproof frequently comes in the form of open (not leading) questions, because questions create the dialogue that invites more penetrating observations.

- *Is my goal to promote God's truth or my preference?* At any point in our marriage, there may be a number of areas in which we would like to see our spouse change. But a good surgeon won't operate just because he doesn't like something about the patient—"Hey, as long as we're at the appendix, let's shave off a few pounds with a tummy tuck!" Our best reproof will come if our goal is to help our spouse hear God's Word, take it to heart, and ultimately respond to it. Our observations should be designed to lead to God's truth, not replace it.

A Good Surgeon Displays Courage

As we've seen, it took considerable wisdom for Nathan to confront David. It also took courage to walk into that palace and speak truth. Reproving a king who had shown himself perfectly willing to kill a man who might discover his sin was a risky move for Nathan—just how risky he couldn't be sure. But the well-being of the nation rode on Nathan's gutsy commitment to say, "You are the one."

Indeed, true biblical wisdom will often have a courageous edge to it, as we walk in faith, seeking to please God in all things. It might seem that life will be easier if we take the timid path of avoiding certain uncomfortable truths or winking at selected sins, but we always reap what we sow (Galatians 6:7–9). If we sow loving honesty and courageous care, we will reap growth in godliness. If we avoid confrontation, we'll just get confrontation anyway, because sin unaddressed is sin unconfined. In an attempt to preserve peace, we sow war.

A second kind of courage is also necessary for the spiritual surgeon. If the first kind is like the boldness needed to begin surgery—running a scalpel across sterilized flesh to open the first incision—the second kind of courage keeps you at work for as long as it takes to finish, and then keeps you caring and engaged through the recovery period as well. This is the courage that commits to staying involved in personal ministry well after we begin to speak.

So often, couples can treat confrontation like a hand grenade— pop the pin, let it fly, and run for cover. But biblical reproof is not some kind of commando raid. It's careful, committed, surgical care for the soul. A good surgeon is committed not only to the operation, but to post-operative care as well. Why does this require courage? Because God's purpose for reproof is not to achieve a hassle-free marriage but to inspire repentance unto godliness. And repentance and change, friends, simply takes time. When sinners say "I do," we must be committed to the entire process of helping each other grow in godliness through life.

Courageous Surgeons Encourage Repentance

In 1517, Martin Luther nailed to a church door in Wittenberg, Germany, what he believed were self-evident truths of Scripture that were being neglected. When the established church of the day failed to engage with Luther over the substance of his claims, it touched off a little controversy generally referred to as the Protestant Reformation. These scriptural truths—theses, as Luther called them—numbered ninety-five. Which one got top billing? "When our Lord and Master Jesus Christ said, 'Repent' [Matthew 4:17], he willed that the whole life of believers should be one of repentance."[5] Luther was confronting a ceremonial and largely heartless system of religious guilt-release. In Luther's mind, informed by God's Word, the proper response of any sinner to the redemptive work of Christ on the cross would be a turning away from sin and self, toward the Savior of our souls—a life of repentance. While the Protestant church grew primarily out of a recovery of the doctrine of justification by faith alone, it still included this essential (and still valid!) insight into how people change.

To truly care for your spouse in the moment of confrontation, your words and manner of delivery must be designed to encourage repentance. The word is often misunderstood, so before you entertain images of your spouse exchanging weekend wear for sackcloth and ashes, let's be clear about what God is looking for.

Repentance is not about being morbidly fascinated with oneself, preoccupied with analyzing every nuance of one's personality, words, and failures. As we learned from Jeremy's example in the last chapter, repentance isn't ultimately about us at all. It's about God. It's becoming so aware of God, his character, and what he has done that we actively seek to turn from sin and pursue righteousness. Part of the gospel's good news (as we will see in the next chapter) is that grace doesn't stop at the cross. It springs from the cross with invasive and endless surgical strength to ensure that we change, that our lives and marriages please God, and that we arrive at our home in heaven in the end (Jude 1:24).

In repentance, we cooperate with God in this marvelous work, playing a crucial part that he expects us to fulfill and gives us the grace to execute. Indeed, we are always invited by God to "work out your own salvation with fear and trembling" (Philippians 2:12), to "put to death therefore what is earthly in you" (Colossians 3:5), to "walk by the Spirit" (Galatians 5:16), and to "renounce ungodliness and worldly passions" (Titus 2:12). Repentance isn't simply wanting change. It is doing change.

I don't want my spouse to be convinced by my earnestness, as if my good intentions could confer any power to change. I want my loved one to turn to God in repentance, if he or she has indeed sinned. I don't want my words to make a spouse feel "caught" in sin, because I don't want to create a temptation to be more concerned with fixing a problem than encountering God. Confrontation is not a "gotcha" event.

I want my spouse to encounter the Holy Spirit, sent to convict the world of sin (John 16:8), and thus to experience the cleansing and faith-inspiring work of godly sorrow over sin. This is what we see in David as the gravity of his sin begins to dawn on him. "I have sinned against the Lord" (2 Samuel 12:13). Paul describes this godly grief to the Corinthians:

> For even if I made you grieve with my letter, I do not regret it—though I did regret it, for I see that that letter grieved you, though only for a while. As it is, I rejoice, not because you were grieved, but because you were grieved into repenting. For you felt a godly grief, so that you suffered no loss through us. For godly grief produces a repentance that leads to salvation without regret, whereas worldly grief produces death.
>
> (2 Corinthians 7:8–10)

According to Paul, feelings of sorrow alone aren't necessarily conviction. We can be sorrowful for many reasons, including selfish ones. We can be sorry for the bad consequences of our sin, sorry we were caught, sorry we lost someone's respect. This kind of worldly grief can't begin to address the true offense of sin, and it can't begin to change us. Only godly grief brings repentance. And only repentance testifies to the surgical effect of God's truth applied to our sinful hearts.

A Good Surgeon Displays Meekness

Meekness is a great gospel word. Jesus said, "Blessed are the meek, for they shall inherit the earth" (Matthew 5:5). Paul said we are to "put on . . . meekness" (Colossians 3:12). And James urges, "Therefore put away all filthiness and rampant wickedness and receive with meekness the implanted word, which is able to save your souls" (James 1:21).

Meekness has nothing to do with being weak or passive. Meekness is power harnessed by love. It is an expression of humility that will not bristle or defend when challenged about motives. In fact, a meek person realizes that he could have selfish motives and must evaluate himself. This fruit of the Spirit helps us govern our anger, restrain our tongue, and maintain our peace. A. W. Tozer said, "The meek man . . . will have attained a place of soul rest. As he walks on in meekness he will be happy to let God defend him. The old struggle to defend himself is over. He has found the peace which meekness brings."[6]

In marriage, to be meek is not to be weak or vulnerable, but to be so committed to your spouse that you will sacrifice for his or her good. A meek person sees the futility of responding to sin with sin.

You've been there. Your spouse says something, whether intentional or not, and it's like a stomach punch to the soul. You feel assaulted, rejected, embarrassed. Immediately a counterattack strategy begins to form in your mind, one that will rival D-Day in its overwhelming impact. You want to load your mouth and pull the trigger. You want to call in a round of devastating insights that decimate your spouse's claim like a well-targeted air assault. You want to unleash a verbal strike force that will take back every inch of lost ground and extract payment for every twinge of wounded pride. You want to leave meekness in a box back at the base, and just go to war.

In chapter six, we talked about how forgiveness willingly absorbs the cost of sin without seeking retaliation or payment. What empowers that kind of heavenly response? Meekness.

The meek person also understands some key biblical principles of communication and applies them in marriage.

130

1) Being annoyed is not an invitation to speak. "The vexation of a fool is known at once, but the prudent ignores an insult" (Proverbs 12:16).
2) A soft answer has more power than a wrathful tongue. "A soft answer turns away wrath" (Proverbs 15:1).
3) Gentle speech encourages life, whether in conversation or in conflict. "A gentle tongue is a tree of life" (Proverbs 15:4).

Finally, all meekness exhibits a common goal. The meek person wants not only to reflect the meekness of Christ (2 Corinthians 10:1) but also to connect one's spouse back to Christ.

What is my agenda, my motivation, in bringing some sin to the attention of my spouse? Often these motivations are less than noble. Dumping anxieties, securing concessions, indulging fears, punishing the one who hurt us—these desires can drive us to speak too quickly and for the wrong reasons. Believe me, I know! But the goal for a surgical conversation is not simply to smooth things over. It is to care for our soul mate and ultimately to connect him or her to God.

Years ago, Kimm and I saw a pattern of conflict emerging from the way I spoke to her when attempting spiritual surgery. I saw my job as persuasion, not connection back to God. I felt the goal was to secure a response rather than simply share my thoughts and entrust her to God. Really, I was using my position, her trust, and my arguing abilities for selfish reasons. Meekness was nowhere to be found.

Your spouse's sin is not first about you. It may affect you, but the most important thing it reveals is your spouse's relationship with God. A meek spouse seeking to help the other will make that relationship with God the first priority. He or she will recognize that the ultimate hope for change lies in a response toward God, not a capitulation to the spouse. That's why the final stage of any correction must be encouraging our spouse toward God and entrusting our spouse to God.

The people we love need to know we are more confident in God's ability to break through than in sin's ability to deceive. God wants to make himself huge in our marriages—so big that our reproof leaves each other more aware of God's activity than of sin's effects. My friend, C. J. Mahaney, calls these *evidences of grace.* "This means actively looking for ways that God is at work in the lives of other people."[7]

Grace is an essential healing agent in the operating room of our sin. It supplies the reason for hope and the power for change. This point is so important that we're going to spend an entire chapter on it, so stay tuned! But before we leave this chapter, consider this: A good surgeon carries the cross right into the operating room. It is the first and last thing he reaches for in surgery. It both opens and closes the patient. Surgery is only successful when we move people beyond their problems to the Great Physician.

Nathan and David Revisited

We've been learning that reproof, like surgery, is difficult to understand and even more difficult to perform. And if performed without wisdom, courage, and meekness, the remedy can seem worse than the problem. But as a husband who has both given and received reproof in a variety of forms, I can tell you this: Few things have been more fruitful for my marriage than the faithful wounds of my friends, especially my best friend Kimm. Let's close this chapter by looking at the ultimate impact of the faithful wounds of Nathan, David's friend, on his king.

Nathan's rebuke did not stop God's discipline of David, but it did prepare him for it. And David's personal journaling of this event has been saved by God for our encouragement in the words of Psalm 51. Here we see a man experiencing the humble clarity of conviction and repentance, a work of God wrought through the faithful rebuke of a friend.

For I know my transgressions,
and my sin is ever before me.
Against you, you only, have I sinned
and done what is evil in your sight,
so that you may be justified in your words
and blameless in your judgment . . .
Behold, you delight in truth in the inward being,
and you teach me wisdom in the secret heart . . .
Hide your face from my sins,
and blot out all my iniquities.
Create in me a clean heart, O God,
and renew a right spirit within me.
Cast me not away from your presence,
and take not your Holy Spirit from me.
Restore to me the joy of your salvation,
and uphold me with a willing spirit.
(Psalm 51:3, 4, 6, 9–12)

Throughout history, men and women of God have gone to David's confession Psalm to find the faith they need to embrace the discipline of God. But what about the rest of the story? What about Nathan and David? Did this reproof damage their relationship, undermine trust? Where did this sovereign encounter leave their friendship?

At the end of David's life, when even his sons were against him, one man stood with him through it all. Nathan, his friend, the surgeon of his soul was there—wise, courageous, and meek, faithful with the truth, and faithful to his friend to the end.

Theirs was a friendship forged in the heat of honest correction. The longer I live the more I cherish the Nathan-like love of my wife, sending me to my Great Physician, full of grace and truth for my time of need. May you welcome the Nathan that the Great Physician has placed in your life through the gift of marriage!

Chapter Eight

Stubborn Grace

Persistent Power to Run Together

I'm way too masculine to enjoy Jane Austen. Now, I realize that women usually read that as, "I'm not smart enough to get Jane Austen," and I suppose there may be some truth to that. But even if guys like me don't get the point, I've got to respect any author who can actually capture the imagination of an audience without mentioning a grenade-launcher. Even once. But I'm still way too masculine to enjoy Jane Austen.

In a touch of divine humor, God has given me a wife and two daughters who love everything Austen-esque. Maybe I'm missing something, but it seems to me that the plot is always the same. The only difference I can see is the name of the mansion.

If you've never read a Jane Austen novel or seen a movie adaptation, let me save you some time. Here's the plot. Start with an anxious, unmarried woman in late eighteenth-century England whose mom is wound up even tighter than she is. Bring in a clueless guy, also usually rich and unexplainably single, who doesn't know he needs the temperamental unmarried woman to make him normal. Throw in some eccentric characters, frilly clothes, a formal ball, and lots of soggy English countryside. End with a deliriously happy wedding, leaving the distinct impression that this couple will never know anything but harmonious marital bliss. Cut to credits, cue the violins, go buy the soundtrack. That about sums it up.

Why doesn't anything happen in Jane Austen after the wedding? What about sequels? Here are a few post-wedding Austen stories I'd like to see:

> *Sense and Sensibility, Episode II—I Miss My Mom*
> *Pride and Prejudice—The Sequel: Darcy's Hunting*
>   *Buddies Move In*
> *Emma Returns: The Matchmaker Strikes Again!*

I know . . . not likely. That's why I prefer guy flicks. They end at the right spot—usually when somebody dies. A Western never ends before the two main characters face off in the street, guns blazing. War movies don't end just as the bombing raid is taking off. And sports movies don't end until you see how the big game turned out. But in the world of Jane Austen, stories end at the altar, just when reality is about to come knocking. I don't get it.

Actually, I do get it. These are romance movies. They're about how the dizzying tornado of romantic love can pick you up in its whirling funnel and set you down at the chapel doors all giddy and beautifully dressed. Where the whirlwind goes from there, no one seems to know. Is there life in fiction after "I do"? Hard to say, since you rarely see a romance movie with married people.

Now, it would be natural in a book on marriage to spring from this illustration to a discourse on how to keep romance alive in marriage. And that's a worthy goal, indeed. (In fact, it's so important that I encourage you to read this endnote to learn about some outstanding material on romance in marriage.)[1] But I have a different purpose in mind. I want to look at a word that can inspire faith and hope when sinners say "I do." The word is *grace*.

Grace is often seen, wrongly, as playing a role much like that of romance in a Jane Austen plot. Grace gets us to the altar with God. It's a mysterious, powerful force that draws us out of our sinful isolation and deposits us into sweet relationship with God through Christ. But once grace saves, the story's over.

You come across this sometimes in salvation testimonies. Great detail is presented about sins committed as an unbeliever. This is followed by God's miraculous intervention, deep joy in the new birth, and then—well, roll the credits. Grace accomplishes the amazing, impossible task of delivering me safely to the altar of conversion, but then it rides off to save someone else, leaving me to fend for myself. Is that really the way it is?

Persistent Grace to Run the Race

A great theologian of our time, J. I. Packer, has observed, "No need in Christendom is more urgent than the need for a renewed awareness of what the grace of God really is."[2] I couldn't agree more. Christians who cultivate an appreciation for God's grace and who seek to apply that grace to every area of their lives, position themselves to know a joyfulness and effectiveness that only God can grant. I also agree that the depth and breadth of God's grace is so poorly understood among Christians that "urgent" is not too strong a word. For married Christians, no area of application could be more urgent than one's own marriage.

Our temptation is to believe that the way to a good Christian marriage is right teaching, right action, working harder, repenting more, and feeling different. Sure, these are crucial, but they are not grace. Again, for you and me there is no more urgent need than a deepening awareness of what the grace of God really means when sinners say "I do." In Titus 2:11–14, Paul takes us beyond our Austen-ish tendency to leave grace at the altar.

v. 11) For the grace of God has appeared, bringing salvation for all people,

v. 12) training us to renounce ungodliness and worldly passions, and to live self-controlled, upright, and godly lives in the present age,

v. 13) waiting for our blessed hope, the appearing of the glory of our great God and Savior Jesus Christ,

v. 14) who gave himself for us to redeem us from all lawlessness and to purify for himself a people for his own possession who are zealous for good works.

These verses carry good news! There is a glorious sequel to saving, justifying grace. The grace that justifies (declaring us holy in God's sight) becomes the grace that sanctifies (making us ever more holy in daily life). It is a prevailing, unstoppable grace that doesn't close up shop the day after the sinner's prayer. It's the power of God to help us overcome sin, and a potent weapon in the fierce struggles that accompany life after the honeymoon of conversion. Conversion, like a wedding, is hardly the end of the story—it's just the beginning!

In these verses, Paul shows us how saving grace becomes sanctifying grace. Let's walk through the passage, looking closely, that we might attain, as Packer puts it, "a renewed awareness of what the grace of God really is."

In verse 11, we see that grace begins with our Savior—the embodiment of grace—appearing and bringing salvation to the lost, reconciliation to the enemies of God. The miracle of his incarnation and the magnificence of his atonement have made salvation a reality. This is the foundation and fountain of grace. Grace appeared in Christ.

Just to clarify, saving grace and sanctifying grace are the *same* grace. The different names just indicate the focus of grace's activity, not that a different *kind* of grace is at work. In fact, when we get to that final day we will clearly see life on this earth as having been all of grace, the same grace of God in and through Christ, grace upon grace, from beginning to end (Zechariah 4:7; Revelation 22:21)! Thus, sanctifying grace is not new grace, or a change in grace. It is grace—the same grace that saved us—applied to the new heart of the child of God, a heart changed by saving grace.

Sanctifying grace is good news. It's the news that God gives *persistent grace to run the race.* It's helpful to view grace this way because it maintains the careful balance Paul is getting at. Paul is not saying that grace effects change in us against our will. Nor is he portraying grace like an energy bar, a timely boost of get-up-and-go when we're a little low in the tank. No, grace is constantly at work in us, gradually and incrementally, so that we can patiently but diligently run the race set out for us. And a significant part of the race we will run is our marriage.

Think about the areas where you know you need to grow— the hair-trigger critical response, the self-pity party, the fermenting anger or discontent. God promises persistent grace to help you run away from that sin and finish well. "Human sin is stubborn," says Cornelius Plantinga, "but not as stubborn as the grace of God and not half so persistent, not half so ready to suffer to win its way."[3] Stubborn, persistent, unrelenting grace that changes us. Now that's good news indeed.

Grace: the Power to Renounce the Old

In verse 12, we discover that the grace of God arrives with a purpose that extends beyond salvation. It comes, "training us to renounce ungodliness and worldly passions, and to live self-controlled, upright, and godly lives in the present age." The grace of God did not simply appear; it brought along a job description. For the Christian, grace is here to teach us how to live in the unique, individual, moment-by-moment lives we all lead.

Where the English Standard Version translates the beginning of verse 12 as "training us," the New International Version expresses it as "teaches us," and the New American Standard reads, "instructing us." This reflects the fact that the Greek word for "training" is complex. It means much more than a knowledge dump from one to another. And it's more than a lesson here and a lesson there, with nothing in between. Grace is a permanent fixture in the life of every Christian, a divine force constantly on the job, a 24/7 truth applier standing over all we do. Grace is the teacher-turned-coach that insists we run toward God.

When I was in Little League, our coach possessed the rare gift of bringing out the best in kids. This was a real challenge given who he had to work with. Coach Hayes was a gruff, often unshaven steelworker whose twin passions, kids and baseball, converged twice a week during the summer—more if there were make-up games.

Coach Hayes had a way about him. He could coax excellence from a skinny right-fielder who found himself holding a glove because his mom wanted him to get some fresh air. And he would teach and train with the full expectation that you would apply what he said. As a result, he took a ragtag group of kids and made them a championship team. It's not that he was given exceptional players, it's that his coaching was excellent. It's not that we were great students of the game. He was a great teacher.

John Stott says, "Now Paul personifies this grace of God. Grace the saviour becomes grace the teacher."[4] Titus 2:12 reminds us that spiritual growth is inevitable, not because we are great students, but because grace is an exceptional teacher. That's how grace works. It's the coach who won't quit, the teacher who never clocks out. Grace is persistent to enable us to run the race.

So, what is the first exercise in our training? Grace trains us to "renounce." That means to deny, reject, or refuse. There are two targets within the crosshairs of grace: ungodliness and worldly passions. Here God reminds us that the biggest challenge in our marriage is that we tend to live more like the old man (or woman) that we once were, than the new man or woman we have become in Christ. But have no fear: God has made provision for change! Grace meets us right where we are, to take us to where God wants us to be. Grace in salvation gave us new desires to please God and live for his glory. Grace in sanctification works to overcome the remaining opposition of sin and move us toward the goal that saving grace has set in our hearts.

This power is very practical. Say your spouse speaks angry words to you, your wife is disrespectful, your husband is cold (or does something dumb like try to hurl the folded clothes up the stairs). Grace arrives to help us renounce the phrases forming in our minds and the passion for punishment erupting within our hearts.

Because grace is of God, it is violently opposed to sin. It instructs us to strangle, mortify, go to war with, and kill sin. Its counsel is simple: lock, load, aim at sin, and pull the trigger. Like a heat-seeking missile, grace locks onto those areas of the old nature and goes to work routing them from our lives. God brings liberation from your sin by showing you areas of ungodliness and empowering you to renounce them, thereby denying sin its satisfaction.

Perhaps there are areas of sin God is exposing in you. If so, his intention is that you renounce them. What are you waiting for?

Grace: the Power to Live

Imagine sitting with a pastor for pre-marital counseling where every piece of advice begins with "don't." Don't criticize her cooking. Don't laugh at how he matches clothes. Don't complain, lie, cheat, or steal . . . don't, don't, don't! I'm all for scriptural "do nots." We need them to help us identify and flee from foolishness and sin. But a deluge of "do nots" won't deliver a great marriage. Maturity comes not just from knowing what to avoid, but what to pursue.

That's why there are two aspects to sanctifying grace: a renouncing and an embracing—a turning *from* what is wrong and a turning *toward* what is right. It's there in the second part of verse 12. It teaches us "to live self-controlled, upright, and godly lives in the present age" (Titus 2:12).

As we practice renouncing sin, sanctifying grace teaches us how to replace the passions of this world with godliness. As a result, we grow in charitable thoughts, patience with our spouse, self-control instead of angry words, love, joy, peace . . . a virtually unlimited array of godly motivations and actions that look increasingly like the character of Christ and combine to make marriage sweet.

Grace: the Power to Wait

I hate to wait. I think fast food is slow, instant coffee is tedious, and instant messages take too long to type. I want to live in a world that runs on my internal clock. Yeah, Dave World, I like that . . . But no, God is in control, not me. So it's good for me that a third component of grace displayed in this passage is the power to wait. We are called "to live . . . in the present age, waiting for . . . the appearing of . . . Jesus Christ."

I took out a lot of words from that passage to emphasize this one point: A hallmark of the Christian life, one of the core things we do as believers seeking to glorify God, is simply to wait. Our marriages play out in a historical waiting room between Jesus' first coming and his final return. Paul calls that waiting room "the present age." In the midst of all the activity, all the turning from sin and turning to godliness, we wait.

How does that work? What's the purpose of having activity and inactivity coexist? What does it mean to act and to wait at the same time? To answer that, let's look at what Paul is telling us in this passage.

Notice the dual focus Paul puts together in a single sentence. One moment he is talking about the clear, tangible, here-and-now realities of daily life (living self-controlled, upright, and godly lives) and the next moment he has leapt ahead to the return of the Lord. What's up with that?

Paul is keeping our hope where it ultimately belongs—in Christ. This life, friends, is not really about you and me at all. It's about God's glory expressed *through* us. In this waiting room, God promises sanctification, a pattern of God-glorifying overall spiritual growth brought about by the power of his persistent grace. But in this life he does not promise to subdue every sin, strengthen every weakness, create unbroken harmony in your marriage, or cure every ailment.

If God fixed everything on the list you have now, don't you think you would just make another list? Then another list, and another after that? What's the end of that process? Perfection, which we don't get in this life. That's why we wait. Perfection is coming. Perfection will arrive when the Son of God returns and we dwell with him in the new heavens and the new earth.

In the present age we cooperate with God's persistent sanctifying grace to live self-controlled, upright, and godly lives. We understand that some sins, challenges, difficulties, and weaknesses may never be totally overcome, and that all change takes time. But because grace is so powerful, thorough, and comprehensive, even this waiting is for our good.

Waiting works things into our souls and our marriages that nothing else can. It's a lesson I have to relearn on a regular basis. When there's an unresolved issue in my marriage that I think demands clarity and resolution *now*, I don't want to hear "trust and wait." I want to hear "do this and watch the problem vanish." I often want change in my marriage to be immediate; I want change in my spouse to be immediate. I want it to be like hitting the delete key on my computer.

But God is not a Mr. Fixit spiritual handyman armed with duct tape and superglue. He is a patient craftsman who lavishes attention on the smallest detail. The creation of character that exhibits godliness and self-control is crafted slowly over time.

Grace interacts with time and eternity. Sanctifying grace settles our souls so that here in this waiting room we can both work and wait, trusting that God is exercising his perfect will, even in those areas where we wait, and wait, and wait. In the end, all the countless waits, large and small, and the hopes that accompany them, are part of our greater waiting and our ultimate hope. As persistent sanctifying grace works in our marriages to make us more *like* Christ, we wait *for* Christ. He is as glorified in our patient waiting as he is in our diligent working.

Grace: the Power to Want

Before Christ, we were committed to worldly passions. We were all exploring and indulging our sinful desires. Zealous for our own way, we were fervent about the wrong things and ardent for sin. But grace has now appeared in Christ to train us and to redirect our passions toward God. We see this at the end of verse 14, where Paul points out that one of God's primary goals in saving us was that we might be "zealous for good works" (Titus 2:14).

What is zeal? Zeal is desire on steroids. An average football fan sits in the stands and cheers, but a zealous one will sit shirtless in subfreezing weather with his body painted in team colors. Zeal is people who get up at 5:00 a.m. on Black Friday to stand in the dark to score a bargain. Zeal is deep desire that defines how we live and reveals what we love.

Grace not only trains. It transforms us from within. Grace excavates all the way down to our core desires and directs them to God. What we want in life actually changes. Grace renovates our zeal and doesn't quit until the good works flow.

Could your marriage be helped by some good works? Maybe things have drifted to a place where even the smallest kindness seems like the biggest step. Perhaps the windows frost over every time you and your spouse find yourselves in the same room. Don't despair, God has sent grace—persistent, sanctifying grace! It can work powerfully in you, not simply to call forth dutiful obedience but to make you "zealous for good works" in marriage.

A grace that transforms us from the inside out. No wonder they call it amazing!

Exporting this Grace

As we prepare to wrap up this chapter, let's take a look at where Paul goes next in his discussion of grace. In verse 15 he continues, "Declare these things, exhort and rebuke with all authority, let no one disregard you." Here, Paul was primarily instructing a pastor named Titus. But you and I as well are called to pass along the word of grace through declaration and exhortation, especially to our spouse. The next time your spouse is struggling in some area, what could it mean for you to declare and exhort using some variation of the following statement:

Dear, the grace of God has appeared to you. Christ has made you his own. His grace supplies you with persistent, effective spiritual power which is training you to renounce ungodliness and worldly passions—right now, even in and through this trial! Let me encourage you to remember this, and act accordingly. Press into God's persistent grace.

How often do you point your spouse back to the grace of God? How often do you remind him or her that God's grace is always at work to train and change us? I don't think I do it enough. Robert Murray M'Cheyne once said, "For one look at yourself, take ten looks at Christ."[5] For that to happen, we need help. It's easy to have our spiritual perspective skewed by paying too much attention to what we see inside. How can we help one another along? Here are four things to keep in mind when encouraging your spouse in the grace of God.

1. Your spouse is inclined to drift from grace to self-effort.

I just need to do more, work harder, give it more effort. We're like the executive who can't delegate because he assumes he has to do it all himself, but whose poor health and bouts of exhaustion tell the real story. Self-effort may make us feel better on some level but it's ultimately futile. When we live more aware of what we need to do than of what Christ has already done, we're drifting—and this is not uncommon, particularly in marriage.

Assume this about your marriage: A key reason God has given you to each other is to apply verse 15—to remind each other of the gospel. I must remind my wife that she needs God in this particular situation or conflict, and that God has power readily available to accomplish his will. This is the kind of exhorting that God calls each of us to do.

Here are some practical steps you can take:

• *Preach the gospel to your spouse.*

Jerry Bridges says, "We need to continue to hear the gospel every day of our Christian lives."[6] The only true antidote to

146

self-effort is to be reminded of how impotent we were to save ourselves. The gospel is the power of God for all life change (1 Corinthians 1:18).

• *Encourage meditation upon the riches of the gospel.*

Our affections follow our meditation, so it is important to explore mind habits, recognize mental ruts, and make truth a regular focus. "The mind is the leading faculty of the soul. When the mind fixes upon an object or course of action, the will and the affections (heart) follow suit. They are incapable of any other consideration . . . The mind's office is to guide, to direct, to choose and to lead."[7]

• *Encourage resting in God even as the battle rages.*

Jesus said, "Come to me, all who labor and are heavy laden, and I will give you rest. Take my yoke upon you, and learn from me, for I am gentle and lowly in heart, and you will find rest for your souls" (Matthew 11:28–29). This promise of rest isn't like an occasional nap or unexpected snow day. It's a reminder that drawing close to Christ continually rejuvenates the soul. Make sure your spouse remembers this!

The secular culture tells us that we're in the driver's seat and everything is really up to us. This is the opposite of what we find in Scripture. God's Word decimates that mindset by reminding us of the absolute power of the grace of God. He then calls us, as Paul called Timothy, to "be strengthened by the grace that is in Jesus Christ" (2 Timothy 2:1).

2. Your spouse may tend to become discouraged.

Can you relate to my impatience with the pace of change? Your spouse probably can too. It's here that we are all vulnerable to discouragement in the fight. The stalled conflict or the child who left orbit long ago and isn't changing—these are opportunities to exercise and model patience even though change isn't happening according to our timetable. It's in these moments we need to remind each other of a persistent grace to run the race.

What if your spouse can't see *any* progress? How can we practically encourage one another when discouragement sets in?

- *Remind your spouse that God works beneath the surface well before change becomes visible.* A seed can be growing even though we see no evidence of growth. Encourage your spouse not to sell grace short. It is working whether we see it or not.

- *Celebrate what you can see, even if it is not directly related to the area of desired change.* Grace should be acknowledged and celebrated wherever it springs up and in whatever form. Sometimes grace is at work where we don't expect it. The husband struggling with lust finds grace to resolve his overeating and then suddenly discovers the power to say no to pornography. The self-critical wife reaches out of her comfort zone to share the gospel with a neighbor and finds her delight in God skyrocketing. Ours is not to dictate the way change should happen, but to be thankful wherever grace becomes evident.

- *Review the game plan for change.* If you're like me, sometimes the game plan is, "Worry first, then pray when it occurs to you." But God has so much more for us! Sit down with your spouse and discuss a strategy together. Ask, "What spiritual disciplines can we bring to bear on this area? Who in our church can we involve for counsel and prayer?" Sometimes grace comes through a simple willingness to take action. When it does, act decisively.

3. Your spouse can lose sight of the ultimate goal.

In our spiritual battles, we can be so aware of the fight to overcome specific sin tendencies that we begin to think the Christian life is basically about dealing with sin. That's completely wrong. Yes, we are called to become ever more effective warriors against sin. But everything we do in this temporary world serves as training for the permanent world yet to come. It's easy to forget that bigger picture.

There is no one more fit to remind us of the ultimate goal of life than the person who is walking toward that goal with us in the bond of marriage.

4. Your spouse must be pointed not to grace, but to the one from whom all grace flows.

When my daughter was about four years old, she decided she was ready to ride her bike without training wheels. My wife and I celebrated that big moment and took her to a big, empty parking lot. We pulled the bike out of the van, took off the training wheels, and placed my daughter on the seat. She was giggling with delight. "I'm ready," she exclaimed. I gave her a little launch and began to instruct, "You've got to pedal, go ahead!" but all the while I kept my hands on the back of the seat. We started going faster, until I was running to keep up. The whole time she's yelling, "Look at me! Look at me! I'm riding my bike!" never really getting it that Dad was holding her up.

That's you and that's me. We roll along thinking we're the reason our marriage is making progress. We can live completely oblivious to the Father behind us, one divine hand on the seat and another on the handlebars. Marriage provides us the opportunity to remind one another of the real power behind our progress and direction. Does your spouse ever become captivated with his or her own pedaling? That's why God gave us each other.

A couple of weeks ago Kimm and I took the kids hiking. It was supposed to be a day of fresh air and exercise amidst the autumn foliage. Instead it became a "Dad can't read the trail map so let's walk around aimlessly for hours" memory. My family has discovered that in order for them to get a Sabbath, I need to go to work.

But in the middle of it all, at an unknown intersection of trails somewhere deep in the woods, I encountered a poignant moment of grace. As it dawned on the group that our location was less than clear, and young minds began to ruminate about flare guns and food rationing, Kimm announced with a smile, "This is great. It gives us extra exercise and allows us to see even more of the trails."

We eventually found our way out. Somehow. But I couldn't stop thinking about Kimm's comment—the way it moved us beyond my mistake to see the good that could result. Slowly a smile spread across my face. When a spouse communicates grace, we move beyond mistakes and the journey becomes enjoyable. That's the way it's supposed to be when sinners say "I do."

Grace—amazing, persistent grace—is helping us each day to run the race of renouncing, living, waiting, and wanting. Jane Austen may have never seen its value, but on an unnamed path in the woods of Pennsylvania, I certainly did. Are you seeing it, too? The grace of God has appeared with a power so stubborn that it will not allow sin to ultimately win. That's remarkable news for the journey of marriage.

Chapter Nine

Concerning Sex

Straight to the Heart
of What Keeps Us Apart

Sex Commands Attention

I don't remember much about my neighborhood Dairy Queen . . . except for THE SIGN. It hung provocatively above the counter, arresting the attention of every teenage boy in search of a Blizzard. Some signs direct, others warn, still others prohibit certain actions, but the headline on this sign was a tractor beam for our attention. It read "CONCERNING SEX." Even gliding past it could melt the ice cream of any adolescent lad.

But the headline was just an attention-getter. The sign wasn't about sex at all. The small print was nothing but an etiquette list for customers. Clever. Yet somehow, every time I came in, I still thought that sign might unlock some secret "CONCERNING

SEX." *Maybe they've added new information.* So I would read it again. Now that I think about it, I don't know if I'd want to learn about sex in a place where everything they sell is frozen. But the point couldn't be more clear: Sex commands attention.

Addressing the topic of sex in marriage can be tricky. Yet the strengths and weaknesses of a marriage are often more obvious in the bedroom than anywhere else. Here's a phrase you may remember from chapter two, "When sin becomes bitter, marriage becomes sweet." The quality of sex can be a fragile thing. Its sweetness is easily soured by the working of sin in our lives. But grace breathes life and faith into every vulnerable area of our marriages—even sex.

But no need to worry about diagrams or graphic descriptions. I intend to be careful, pastoral, and practical. I want to help you apply God's Word to this very area. And I want to hold out hope. Even if this is an area of frustration, contention, or despair, God wants to ignite fresh sparks of faith in your marriage for a mutually enjoyable sexual experience. God created sex to be satisfying within marriage. The whole thing was his idea.

When I was a kid at the Dairy Queen, sex commanded attention for all the wrong reasons. But in the Bible, sex in marriage commands attention for the right reasons. As a magnificent gift bestowed by our Creator, sex is given to be celebrated. But the impact of this remarkable gift does not stop with us. Marriages that are sexually satisfying in private carry into the public sphere a certain sparkle, an open demonstration of joy and unity that helps point people to the Creator of marriage. When God says, "concerning sex," it really is worth looking at the fine print.

A Biblical Ice-Breaker

To begin the discussion let's tiptoe beyond our discomfort and hear what our Creator has to say on the subject. Who will break the ice? Enter Paul, Theologian of the Uncomfortable Topic. Once again, God uses this brave man to speak grace to us in a very vulnerable area. Here's what Paul has written on his own sign "CONCERNING SEX . . ."

> Now concerning the matters about which you wrote, "It is good for a man not to have sexual relations with a woman." But because of the temptation to sexual immorality, each man should have his own wife and each woman her own husband. The husband should give to his wife her conjugal rights, and likewise the wife to her husband. For the wife does not have authority over her own body, but the husband does. Likewise the husband does not have authority over his own body, but the wife does. Do not deprive one another, except perhaps by agreement for a limited time, that you may devote yourselves to prayer; but then come together again, so that Satan may not tempt you because of your lack of self-control.
>
> (1 Corinthians 7:1–5)

Paul did not send these commands to a church or society that was neutral on the subject of sex. Never one to ignore the elephant in the room, Paul spoke into a culture known for its moral corruption. At the time he wrote these words, Corinth was infamous for sexual sin. In Greek culture, the verb to *corinthiazethai* came to represent gross immorality and drunken debauchery.[1] John MacArthur writes, "The sexually corrupt, the covetous, swindling and idolatrous people to whom Paul referred were fellow church members who refused to give up, or had fallen back into, the debauched lifestyle of Corinth."[2] This church was scandalized with perversion. Sex was clearly quite popular . . . except perhaps in marriage.

But problems were opportunities for the great apostle. Instead of bowing under the pressure to overlook the Corinthian church's "lifestyle choices," Paul brought clarity to the controversial issue of sexuality. He placed sex under the gracious concern of the holy God. In a culture of polygamy, homosexuality, divorce-on-demand, and over-the-top sexual indulgence, this was no small adjustment. Paul was concerned about behavior, but he was focused on the heart—what truly determines how we relate to sex, both inside and outside of marriage. Reading 1 Corinthians leaves no doubt: God cares about sexuality—and he cares as much about its proper expression as he does its improper expression. We already know more than we need to know about the second category. It's time we focused on the first.

With Scripture opening the door to honest discussion about sexuality in marriage, I'd like to post a variation on the CONCERNING SEX sign. The headline on this one reads "SEX IN MARRIAGE IS AN ADVENTURE." I hope that gets your attention, and I promise to follow it up with material far more relevant than tips on being a conscientious fast-food diner.

I want to discuss some implications for sex which I believe root themselves in Paul's challenge to the Corinthians—the challenge to married couples concerning rights and responsibilities, and the causes and effects of both intimacy problems and intimacy breakthroughs. It's a discussion in which we will come to see sexuality in marriage as an adventure of Devotion, Delight, and Dependence.

Let's Talk

At the end of each adventure section I'm going to offer some simple ways you and your spouse can talk about the point being made. Why? Well, because there may be no area more thought about and less talked about in a marriage than sex. But marriage is a call to oneness—and oneness requires communication. This is why R. C. Sproul has written, "Sexual communication in marriage is imperative."[3] While it can be difficult to start, couples who have worked at openly talking about their fears and expectations around sex find not only a richer love life, but a deeper, more trusting marriage.

Sex in Marriage is an Adventure of Devotion

If the mention of "devotion" in the context of sex seems odd to you ("Of course he's going to talk about being devoted to sex. He's a man isn't he!"), please hear me out. By devotion I don't mean a mindless, dutiful, my-spouse-is-really-needy-so-I-guess-I'd-better-deliver mentality. My goal is the same as Paul's: to re-order some basic ideas we have about sex.

Devotion to one another's protection

In 1 Corinthians 7:2, Paul describes the protective purpose of sex in marriage, "Because of the temptation to sexual immorality, each man should have his own wife, and each woman her own husband."

For the Christian, sex in marriage is to be a God-installed defense against temptation. Our world is like Corinth, always advertising sex outside of marriage as if it delivers nothing but sweet, illicit adventure. Husbands are targeted by a pornography industry boasting millions of websites and spam that is constantly reprogrammed to bypass email filters and firewalls.[4] Publishers and producers have wives in their crosshairs as they churn out new romance novels and daytime soap operas. We live in a sex-obsessed society—no debate there. The ways society plays on lust changes from culture to culture, but the temptation is universal—and potentially overwhelming.

How can married Christians be protected from this ever-growing sexual onslaught? By God's faithful provision through marriage—your protection sleeps right next to you every night. Marriage exists for many wonderful reasons, some of them mysterious and some intensely practical. This matter of protection is of the intensely practical variety. Our spouse is our first line of defense to protect us from the calls of Corinth.

Most couples with a healthy sex life live largely unaware of how much their physical relationship works silently but powerfully against sexual temptation. Recently the tailpipe on our car broke. I never think about tailpipes. I don't ever remember thanking God for one. They just sit there under the car, silently working their subtle magic by protecting us from noxious fumes and obnoxious noise. When one breaks, though, everyone knows it and driving becomes a different experience. Depressing the accelerator produces an outrageous series of noises. People look at you funny in parking lots. Pausing at a long stoplight raises the specter of the entire family suffering carbon monoxide poisoning. A functioning tailpipe works silently but powerfully to protect us from some serious problems.

And in marriage, it is sex that protects. Sex works invisibly but powerfully to diminish temptations to sexual immorality. We need to see that such moral protection is not just a pleasant byproduct of marital intimacy. It is a core reason *for* marital intimacy.

Marital sex (which glorifies God, honors marriage, and satisfies spouses) exists in part to prevent adultery (which insults God, betrays marriage, and debases spouses). When we deprive our spouse of the adventure of sexual devotion, we leave him or her unprotected, open to physical and emotional temptations that can leave marriage vulnerable to destructive actions and habits. In our culture of self-fulfillment this protective aspect of sexual intimacy has been obscured by a focus on sexual pleasure. But the Bible doesn't separate protection from pleasure. Both are expressed in the wisdom of sexual relationship in marriage.

Let's Talk

Do you have a basic understanding of where your spouse might face temptation for physical or emotional intimacy outside your marriage? Guys, is your wife aware of how your eyes can be tempted at the beach? Ladies, is your husband aware of how romance movies or shows can tempt you to discontentment in your marriage? We all have vulnerabilities, and we're meant to be helpers to one another in the resistance and battle with them. Let's talk about temptation.

Devotion to one another's rights

In verse three Paul continues, "The husband should give to his wife her conjugal rights, and likewise the wife to her husband." Verse four gives the reason: we don't belong to ourselves.

We can only imagine how these ideas hit the Corinthians: Sex begins and ends with a husband and wife; each has a right over the other; our bodies are not our own . . . WOW! Talk about unenlightened. To a culture that saw the uninhibited indulgence of personal pleasure as both normal and a virtue, acknowledging the value of another person's "body rights" as essential to monogamous marriage must have seemed preposterous.

But marriage becomes an adventure by underscoring the other-centered nature of our union. Marriage means that our bodies are now claimed by God for the pleasure and service of another. Our connection is so comprehensive that God gives our spouse a claim over our body. It's a remarkable picture of the actual scope of "the two becoming one flesh." We are called by God to become devoted to sexually satisfying our spouse.

Let's stop for a heart-check. I recognize there will be some reading this who can't imagine the kind of physical relationship Paul indicates. For you, intimacy with your spouse may be intertwined with a sense of apprehension, rejection, or shame. This is a real challenge in many marriages that cannot be simply overlooked.[5] But let's not think about that problem yet. Let's ponder first the reality of what God holds out for us. God's vision for our sex life is wonderful and intoxicating, and before we can fully experience it we must try to understand and savor it.

Of course, as God's children we are responsible to live according to his words. And as God's *married* children we are responsible also to order our *marriages* according to his words. That is, we live devoted lives to God by living devoted lives toward others. And in the marriage relationship, no one else matters more than your spouse. Paul simply takes the biblical theme of service and applies it to sexual intimacy. In doing so he reminds us that we serve our spouse with our sexuality in two ways: protection from sexual temptation, and the giving-over of conjugal rights.

Let's Talk

Many couples wrestle with frequency in sex, each spouse having different expectations about what a fulfilling sex life should look like. Discuss what your personal ideals of frequency would be—see how close you are to each other. Talk about the distractions or discouragements that can make sex more of an afterthought than a priority for you. Seek as a common goal how to build your schedule and environment in such a way that you can faithfully give to one another "conjugal rights."

Sex in Marriage is an Adventure of Delight

As I write this chapter, about a week before Christmas, I'm really looking forward to our family gift-giving on Christmas morning. When I was a kid, I approached Christmas with an obsession, practically salivating over what I was going to get and the adventure of opening all my wonderful new stuff. But my perspective has changed through the years. Somewhere along the way, I'm not sure when, I discovered it really is better to give than receive. While I am grateful for the gifts my family gives me, my main delight and anticipation at Christmas is in bringing joy to my wife and children—a husband and father blessing his family simply for the pleasure it brings them.

This is a fundamental reality of marriage too. God intends for *our* greatest joy in marriage to come from being a primary source of joy *to our spouse*. John Piper says, "The reason there is so much misery in marriage is not that husbands and

158

wives seek their own pleasure, but that they do not seek it in the pleasure of their spouses."[6] God has designed the sexual relationship as a key expression of this reality, for when sex is at its best, my delight in and enjoyment of sex is almost indistinguishable from the pleasure experienced by my spouse. The joy of sex, then, is the pleasure derived from giving our spouse his or her conjugal rights. Notice Paul doesn't emphasize taking *from* our spouse *our* conjugal rights. By instead emphasizing the giving of these rights to one another, Paul locates the key for great sex as generosity.

Do you know what makes this a real adventure? Most of us come into marriage totally unprepared for it. No matter what our previous experience, newlyweds are meant to arrive at their wedding night viewing themselves as complete novices in the adventure of biblical sex. Ideally, the sexual relationship in marriage then becomes a journey of figuring out how to delight my spouse with my body. And you know what? That adventure remains for as long as you both shall live. It's unaltered by kids, age, or bodies that have broken out of their previous contours.

C. J. Mahaney said, "Indeed any married person who rightly sees these verses as commands from God will bring to the marriage bed a servant's mindset that places the primary emphasis on the sexual satisfaction of his or her spouse."[7] This is part of what makes marriage delightful—the joy of living for someone beyond ourselves.

Self-centeredness in sexual matters, including depriving one another (as Paul warns the Corinthians), is common, because apart from the activity of grace, we are self-centered in everything we do. But there is another way available to us. If you are depriving your spouse of intimacy, or pursuing selfishness in your marriage bed, God wants to get your attention, for he has something far better for you. Many of us shut down when wounded, or withdraw when discouraged, or are tempted to manipulate our spouse by using the body as a bargaining tool.

We can be tempted with "solo sex" through fantasy, pornography, and/or masturbation. These are common temptations, but not at all out of the reach of God's grace. He always provides a way of escape for any temptation (1 Corinthians 10:13), and for you the road to escape from sexual temptation leads eventually and inevitably to your spouse.

And do you know what? If spouses are committed to one another's pleasure, nobody goes to sleep disappointed. I don't have to be concerned with getting *mine*, because my spouse is thinking of adventurous ways to enjoy what God has given *us*. And when someone is intent on getting their delight by being a delight . . . well, it just doesn't get much better than that!

Have I strayed from Paul's point to the Corinthians? I don't think so. He could have made a very different point by saying, "Folks, this sex thing is just too hot for you to handle without sin, so you need to just find a way to minimize its influence in your marriage." But he does the opposite. He pushes husband and wife toward one another, specifically for sex!

Think about the grace that pours from this passage. God cares about us so much that he offers his loving guidance into even the most intimate areas of life. His wisdom is not used up by the big picture items like managing the universe. God reaches down into creation, right into our bedrooms and says, "Can we talk about your sex life with your spouse?" "Let's chat about whether it's all I designed it to be, because I want you to experience delight in one another!" God cares about these things, and he offers us the grace to enjoy fully the adventure of mutual marital delight.

The joy that springs from pleasing our husband or wife is one reason sex was never designed to be a solo pursuit. Biblical sex, with its joyful service and the matchless intimacy born from it, is a glorious expression of what we are intended to be—male and female, created in God's image to enjoy intimacy of relationship in its deepest possible expression. That's a gift I'll take any day!

Let's Talk

Have you ever openly shared with your spouse what brings you pleasure? Is there anything you're experiencing in your sexual relationship that inhibits your pleasure or is even unpleasant? Recognize that sexual preferences are like appetites for food, i.e., nobody is exactly alike. It might be difficult at first, but the more you are able to be graciously truthful in discussing what you like, the more you will educate your spouse, and help them enjoy your time together even more.

Sex in Marriage is an Adventure of Dependence

Although delighting in sex should be the overflow of love in Christian marriages, not every encounter will be accompanied by fireworks or become a contender for your top-ten list of romantic moments. Adventure implies discovery, and wrapped up in the very nature of discovery is an element of unpredictability.

On one occasion Kimm and I arranged for a romantic getaway at a mountain resort. Dressed in high style, we arrived there anticipating a romantic dinner for two. When the hostess showed us our table, we couldn't help noticing that four other couples were already seated . . . at our table! Talk about an adventure. I sat next to a guy who somehow thought what I needed was a play by play of his life story. Now I believe in lifestyle evangelism, but this guy was seriously misjudging my mission that night. Kimm and I have come to expect these little distractions to our romantic pursuits—the traffic jams that make getting to the concert a NASCAR adventure, the "I've never seen a baby throw up so much" phone calls from the sitter—you know what I'm talking about. We used to wonder if God was against romance. Now we know he just likes to create funny stories to go along with it.

Marriage at the level of simple day-to-day details is an adventure all by itself. Add in sex and romance and it becomes an epic quest. To thrive in this lifelong journey, we must see God as more than a comforting touchstone or a helpful guide. He is the center, the one in whom "we live and move and have our being" (Acts 17:28). We are called to depend on him at every moment and in every area—including our sex life.

One of the first things we learn about sex in marriage is how fragile it is. Early in marriage, many couples who "burned" with anticipation of nightly connubial bliss find that sex can easily take a back seat to the pressures and distractions of life. You know the inventory: the over-taxed schedule, the To Do list, health issues, stress, relational distance, "same old, same old" routines in the bedroom, physical dysfunction—these are just a few of the more common reasons sex can become an also-ran in marriage.

Oh yeah . . . kids. Almost forgot that one. Nothing makes you feel less like a lover than living like a parent.

But God's Word speaks to us: real people in real life—not characters in romance movies or sexual Olympians. Scripture brings sound wisdom for the daily experience of marriage, where real people have real problems and need real help from a real God. And that's a good thing because sex, as you probably know, can complicate things, particularly when "things" in the marriage aren't going too well. In those seasons, we especially need God's help to guide us beneath surface misunderstandings to the root problem.

For years we had an oven that couldn't make up its mind. One day Kimm would set it on 550 degrees and food would still take hours to cook. The next day she would pop in a turkey, set the oven on low, and the bird would be carbon in thirty minutes. Dinner was always an adventure. Turned out that the problem was not with the dials but on the inside. Finding the true source of a problem is certainly important when cooking dinner. But it's absolutely critical when you are trying to understand the problems that keep us apart in marriage. Techniques and fresh ideas can sometimes help, but it might surprise you to discover that most sexual problems among married people are rooted in the heart. It's worth taking the time to discover them. Like checking out our oven, the wise couple looks inside when temperature becomes a problem.

Let's look now at sloth, unbelief, and bitterness, three common sins that can rob sweetness from the sexual relationship in marriage.

Sloth

Sloth is a romance killer. Even the word chills the air. By sloth I simply mean laziness with respect to marital intimacy. The most common fruits of this heart condition are passivity and unresponsiveness. We begin to let our appearance go. We grow comfortable with bedroom boredom. We tolerate a lack of sexual desire and settle for one partner doing all the initiating.

Sometimes sexual sloth comes from being busy with the wrong things. A guy who regularly works very long hours can actually be slothful if his choices about where to spend his time and energies leave no room for romancing his wife. How can hard work be sloth? Because a Christian husband is called to make sure he is regularly romancing his wife. If romance and intimacy are being pushed off the schedule too often, he needs to make what may be the more difficult decision: to set work aside and pursue his spouse.

The book of Proverbs illustrates a core attribute of the lazy person, the "sluggard" in wisdom language. "As a door turns on its hinges, so does a sluggard on his bed" (Proverbs 26:14). This is a tragically comic picture of someone who habitually turns away from responsibility in favor of ease. Do you and your spouse turn away from each other when it comes to sex because it doesn't seem worth the time or energy? Don't depend on yourself. Turn toward God and depend on his power to enliven your desire and strengthen your resolve to overcome the eroding effects of sloth on sex.

Unbelief

This chapter is devoted to shoring up belief in God's promises for the sexual relationship in marriage. But when we allow unbelief to tangle its roots around our hearts, we begin to believe its lies. "I can't enjoy sex." "Things will never change." "The past will always bother me." "I can't meet his expectations." "I can't please her."

Or perhaps the lies are aimed at your spouse. "You can't understand me." "You can't meet my needs." "You don't know what it was like to be raised in my home." "You don't understand that when you touch me I think about him touching me." "You can't understand all the baggage I bring."

I'm not talking about the normal questions and doubts we face in times of difficulty. I'm talking about an approach to sex that says, in effect, this is simply beyond God's reach. For whether spoken or unspoken, each of these lies ultimately point heavenward. "God can't answer this prayer." "His promises can't apply to my situation." "God can't change my desire." "I can't trust God." "Grace can't reach this far."

Brothers and sisters, this type of unbelief is devastating, not only to our sex lives, but to our entire spiritual existence. It calls into question the very nature of God (Hebrews 11:6) and places our own feeble, inconsistent selves at the center of reality.

There is also another kind of unbelief, somewhat less blasphemous but equally serious and damaging. It's a faithlessness that says, "I suppose God can help with our sex life, but I can't imagine he actually cares very much." Faith for finances? Sure. Faith for witnessing? You bet. Faith for my job?

164

No problem. But faith for sexual intimacy can feel selfish or frivolous—shouldn't I be engaging with God about something spiritual? It can feel like we have wandered into areas where God prefers not to go.

We must battle both forms of unbelief with a dependence on who God has revealed himself to be in his Word. Scripture tells us that we serve an omnipotent and sovereign God who views sex as central and vital to the closest relationship two people can have.

Bitterness

Bitterness differs from unbelief merely in the intensity and depth—in the degree—of its rebellion. As my friend Andy Farmer has pointed out, the two are distinguished simply by the difference between can't and won't. Unbelief says, "I can't do this," while bitterness says, "I won't do this." Unbelief tells a spouse, "You can't change," and bitterness declares, "You won't change." Unbelief claims, "God can't affect what I like and dislike"; while bitterness says, "God won't affect them."

Unbelief leans away from God's promises; bitterness slams the door. "You defrauded me, and I won't trust you." "You didn't exercise self-control before we were married; you won't after."

Bitterness is one of the most common causes of neglected sex. From the soil of anger and unresolved conflicts, it grows quickly into a virulent weed that chokes out intimacy. Married people turned bitter use their bodies as a weapon, a weapon that harms by withholding. A weapon used to punish the other person for sinning against us. This calls for forgiveness.

Sloth, unbelief, and bitterness are common but serious sins that deny the truth of the gospel. When we cast off God's truth and embrace lies, our marriages and our faith suffer together. But we need not, must not, tolerate these paralyzing patterns of sin. Instead, let us look for them, admit it whenever we find them, and seek God for forgiveness and the power to repent and change.

Daily Dependence: When Sinners say "Woo"

The Adventure of Dependence isn't simply grace to say no to things that hinder our intimacy; it's grace to create an environment where sexual intimacy flows from romance. This kind of grace dependence doesn't occur with a "roses at Valentine's Day, dinner for your birthday" predictability. Nor does it occur with the grand, expensive but infrequent displays of acknowledgement. The adventure of dependence is a daily opportunity to love your spouse in the creative thoughtfulness that says, "You matter to me more than any other person alive."

You may know the story. A man asked his wife what she'd like for her birthday. She replied wistfully, "I would really love to be ten again." On the morning of her birthday, he woke her up early with a bowl of her favorite cereal from when she was a kid. He then whisked her away to a popular theme park for an indescribable day. Cotton candy, hot dogs, roller coaster, the Death Slide—everything there was. She staggered from the theme park, head pounding and stomach nauseous. Straight away he drove her to McDonald's for a Happy Meal with extra fries and a refreshing chocolate shake. Next it was off to the cinema to see the latest blockbuster movie, and of course, M&M's, popcorn, the works. At the end of the day, his wife wobbled home and collapsed exhausted onto the bed. As he stood in the doorway with a big dopey grin, he said "Well, darling, what was it like to be ten again?" The only words mumbled by his wife?

"I meant my dress size."

Ladies, trust me, if you haven't had a similar experience of misguided initiative from your husband, you may be likely to have one in the future. I like this story because it shows a man *doing something creative* to woo his wife. For husbands and wives, the adventure of dependence inevitably leads to the adventure of creative investment.

For those who enjoy few things more than a perfectly scheduled, predictable day, the word creativity may send a shudder of horror down the spine. But we're not talking about painting a landscape or writing a sonata. When it comes to your marriage, think of creativity as simply faith-inspired work, a natural outgrowth of your belief that God cares about your marriage and wants to help you improve it. The important thing is not how naturally creative or imaginative you may be, but whether you truly are walking in dependence on God in improving your marriage. As Gary and Betsy Ricucci have written, "There's no such thing as a romance expert or passion professional. Romance must be continually practiced, like an art".[8]

I've had the privilege of growing in the faith with some unusually gifted people, and I would say it's the rare person for whom creative, romantic ideas come spontaneously. Most of the folks I know pursuing romance and intimacy in their marriages are spending time planning, asking questions, investigating what is romantic to their spouses and not assuming they know. As with any artistry, there are far more discarded ideas than masterpieces. But to get a masterpiece you must be willing to work at creativity. I'll guarantee you this, if you see someone who is truly good at romancing his or her spouse, you probably won't be looking at a natural. You'll be looking at someone who works at creativity, and makes careful planning look effortless. That, my friends, is art worth pursuing.

Great sex in marriage comes from conscious dependence on the goodness and sovereignty of God, who is at work powerfully to make our marriages a source of spiritual and physical joy.

Let's Talk

Ask your spouse whether he or she is aware of sloth, unbelief, or bitterness as a potential obstacle to a God-glorifying sex life. If that is the case, take time to talk about it with the goal of confessing any sin, asking for and receiving forgiveness, and walking in reconciliation. Also, consider expressing your dependence on God for this area of your life by praying together about it. Now for some of you that might be a mental train wreck—prayer and sex at the same time?! But as we have seen, sex is a gift from God, to be received gratefully and stewarded faithfully. So prayer can be a totally appropriate part of your sex life, and just may be a missing ingredient.

Daily Dependence: When Sinners Say "Wow"

My hope in this chapter is to bring the sensitive issue of sex under the hope of the gospel, where it belongs. In one sense I'm transporting us back to the original marriage, when God brought Adam and Eve together to be "helpers" to each other in ways that went far beyond tending the garden. It has been well documented that Adam's response at the first sight of Eve can be faithfully translated as "Wow!" Adam's response tells us much about the joy of sex as God created it to be between a husband and wife in the covenant of marriage. The curse took away the "Wow" and left us with a "woe." Praise be to God, the gospel has undone the curse of sin, and given sinners who say "I do" a way back from "woe" to "Wow!" No matter where we are in our marriages, let's start working together toward that end. And let's look for the day when the sign we put over our marriage bed is,

Concerning Sex? . . . WOW!

Chapter Ten

When Sinners Say Goodbye

Time, Aging, and Our Glorious Hope

write this knowing that if you've gotten this far you've probably spent a good deal of time thinking about things you may never have thought about before. Perhaps you feel the same way I do, that we've been walking together on some less traveled paths. We've walked together up the dizzying inclines of doctrine and into the shadowy depths of self-examination. Our path has taken us into wide open meadows of mercy and grace, and along the unexpectedly rocky terrain of confession and forgiveness. My greatest hope is that, wherever we've walked, we've never lost sight of the cross—the only sure marker for marriage when sinners say "I do." Before we end, I'd like to take you on one more stroll, once again to a place you might not expect.

169

Cemeteries have always factored into my life in a strange way. As a kid fleeing adult supervision, a nearby graveyard was the place for me and my buddies to lay low while the heat from our shenanigans blew over. Later Kimm and I lived right around the corner from a cemetery. People generally don't hang out in such places. There's no picnic area, no playground, no Starbucks. You only go there, well, if you need to. I used to walk with our kids through the big quiet neighborhood cemetery so we could look at the tombstones together. That may sound like an odd way of bonding with one's offspring, but I wanted to impress upon them that today matters because tomorrow can't be assumed. Even kids need to learn about the brevity of life.

Sometimes I have come upon a cemetery plot with a matched pair of headstones, one inscribed, the other still blank. That's when I stop and ponder the marriage story being illustrated there. In my mind's eye I see a young couple, intoxicated by romance, standing wide-eyed at the altar . . . then holding one newborn baby, and another . . . memories and images of a lifetime together. Now one spouse lies here, the other stands alone.

But hold on—before you toss this book aside, muttering "The other chapters were okay but this one is shaping up to be pretty depressing," hear me out. Part of living in a fallen world is suffering the ultimate consequence of Adam's sin—Death. The studies are conclusive. Among those born, all die. There are no special passes and no one is exempt. (Okay, I'm leaving out Enoch and Elijah. But if nobody else—Isaiah, John the Baptist, the twelve Apostles, Paul—got to skip the dying part, you and I aren't exactly leading candidates.)

Indeed, Scripture sets forth an unfashionable goal for believers: God wants us to die well. This has nothing to do with estate-planning. It speaks of whether, through sanctification, our souls are prepared for the inevitable reality of death. The youth-fixated, pain-averse, escapist nature of western culture

170

is an anomaly in human history. Here, preparation for death seems morbid. But throughout history, and in most of the world today, death has always been part of life and deserving of attention. The Puritans, in their admirable "Let's bring God into every moment" perspective, saw marriage as not simply a great way to live, but as a training ground for what lay beyond. Pastor Richard Baxter saw one of the goals of marriage as this, "To prepare each other for the approach of death, and comfort each other in the hopes of life eternal."[1]

Of course, death rarely comes to a husband and wife at the same time. You and your spouse have been joined together, but you probably won't leave together. As D. A. Carson soberly reminds us, "All we have to do is live long enough, and we will be bereaved."[2]

He's got a point there. What about when "death do us part" actually happens? Moses prayed in Psalm 90, "The years of our life are seventy, or even by reason of strength eighty . . . they are soon gone, and we fly away." Moses saw that time passes quickly, and with it go husbands, wives, and marriages. Does our view of marriage ignore this inevitability, or assume it?

Sinners Say "I Do" For the Time of Decline

I grew up playing sports. I loved sports too much, really. As I got older, I still ran regularly for years. Now I have a rogue knee and a rebellious back. They're like a street gang among my members, daring me to make a false move so they can dust me. As much as my pride hates to admit it, this body is on the downhill slide. So now instead of running, I walk (not too much of an athletic feat to brag about around the office). I'm wondering if this whole thing is headed toward crawling for exercise.

I think Paul could relate. He encourages the Corinthians by saying, "So we do not lose heart. Though our outer nature is wasting away, our inner nature is being renewed day by day"

(2 Corinthians 4:16). While describing himself, Paul offers a pretty accurate diagnosis for us as well. This inevitable wasting away comes from our forefather Adam, whose turn from God toward self-sufficiency doomed us to the universal physical destiny of ashes to ashes, dust to dust. Life involves bodily decay, folks. The only question is when do we recognize it.

But Paul overlays this cold physical reality with radiant gospel truth. Bodily decay isn't the only thing going on: We are also being gloriously renewed from within. You see, the new birth, the biblical concept of regeneration, isn't like the old birth. Under the old, physical birth, we basically start dying as soon as we leave the womb. (Talk about peaking early.) But under the new spiritual birth, the life of God re-animates our sin-dead souls and the process is reversed—we actually get *better* with time!

What's going on inside us spiritually is really quite amazing. Our souls are being prepared for eternity with God. This is why Paul tells us not to lose heart. Sure, physically, things aren't so great. Whatever we may have counted as physical assets are quickly becoming liabilities. Faces are showing lines, hair is graying or falling out, muscles are sagging, and midsections are growing. I see it in the mirror every day! Married couples in their early years often talk wistfully of growing old together—trust me, it's harder than it looks.

So when life comes at you in ways you don't expect, remember this: Regeneration is the initial burst of spiritual life in our souls. Renewal is that same power working itself out in every facet of who we are, fitting us, as it were, for eternal life with Jesus.

A Story of Renewal: Mark and Carol

Mark and Carol's married life was complicated. They met in college, fell in love, and began their first year of marriage. But as newlyweds, Carol fell into times of profound discouragement and Mark was having a hard time adjusting to his role as husband. He spent a lot of time with his friends, either playing sports or watching it on TV. According to Mark, he and Carol were more like singles who happened to be married.

Mark pointed the finger at Carol, "I thought she was the one with all the problems . . . so I just continued to pull away." Mark's job required him to spend a lot of time with women. He says, "My affections were being pulled away from Carol; I was having emotional affairs with other women." Eventually Mark and Carol sought help, and a counselor suggested an exercise: go home and write three reasons why you married each other, then talk about it. "It was the hardest assignment I had ever been given," Mark recalls.

As they sat and shared their lists with each other, God broke in and Mark saw, with startling clarity, the depths of his selfishness and irresponsibility. "I broke at this point," Mark remembers. "The Lord began to restore my vision for my marriage and love for Carol in that very moment."

Through confession and repentance, God launched a renewal in Mark's heart. It would eventually sweep over every part of his marriage. It would also prepare him for some disastrous news.

Care for the Clay in Decay

Every married person is united to a mate in decay. "Treasure in jars of clay" is what Paul calls us (2 Corinthians 4:7). It's a visual that fits well, whether you are on the engagement side of the wedding or stacking up anniversaries by the decade. And caring for clay is part of the calling of marriage. We have the joy of preparing one another for heaven even as earth makes its claim on the body. We enjoy front-row seats to the inner renewal even as we see the container wasting away.

173

As Mark and Carol's marriage began to thrive, little did they know there was a storm gathering in Carol's body. Strange symptoms began to appear: tingling in her hands and toes, problems with her eyesight. It seemed serious, and a doctor's visit confirmed their fears. Carol was diagnosed with chronic, progressive multiple sclerosis (MS). The deterioration of the clay jar began soon thereafter. First, Carol walked more slowly. Then she needed a cane. Then she moved to a wheelchair. Then to a bed. And it all happened with crushing suddenness.

But something far more significant was happening as well—renewal. Though Carol's health was decaying, her soul was freshly alive to God and her husband was experiencing a complete renovation. Mark says, "By the time the MS began to show, the Lord had already begun to turn my heart toward Carol. The diagnosis came at almost the same time as the breakthrough in our marriage. MS had affected Carol's sight, motor skills, features, mobility—it seemed that nothing lay untouched. But I had fallen in love again with Carol. I only saw how beautiful she was to me."

Carol has now been bed-bound for twelve years. To her friends and family she is a letter from Christ written in frail human form. On the rare occasions when Carol can go out, Mark tries to seize the chance to do special things with her. The wheelchair she uses when out of bed is designed to keep her lying down. It's quite a feat of engineering. But Mark hardly sees the chair. He's too in love with the woman in it.

Don't Lose Heart

A maturing marriage is one that sees all the way to the finish line and beyond. As married Christians, God bestows upon us the extraordinary honor of nurturing and celebrating the inner renewal while also caring for the outer decay. It's an adventure in irony, made possible by the gospel, the only real treasure in our brittle jars of clay. Not every married Christian sees this clearly. But joy awaits those who do.

Recently, Mark surprised Carol with a date to the Sweethearts Banquet at their local church. This is an event they both love, and Mark had something special in mind. During a slow dance, Mark made his way toward Carol, grabbed her chair and began to dance with her. He just kept turning her around in the chair and telling her how much he loved her. It was a profound moment for Mark, Carol, and everyone there as the crowd parted to make room for the lovers at the center of the dance floor.

From an earthly standpoint, things for Carol are worse than ever. Her health deteriorates and, apart from divine intervention, she will die from complications related to her condition. Mark understands this, but he also feels a deep sense of honor at being able to care for his wife for as long as he has her. Mark says, "I see it as a privilege and honor to serve Carol this way. It does have difficulties, but it is God's way of showing me how much he loves me. I sense his love *for* me in how he has entrusted Carol *to* me."

Mark and Carol are two of my heroes. In their extraordinary, prolonged trial, they are preparing each other for another world by the way they live in this one. Every once in a while, God breaks in on them to sweeten their taste for what is to come. "There are days," Mark says, "when Carol and I sit and pray together and it's like walking on holy ground. We sense the presence of God and we just know he is with us. I think those moments are a little taste of heaven for us."

One day, you or I may be called upon to do something similar for our spouse. Should that opportunity come, will we recognize it as God's love for us, entrusting to us a suffering spouse to care for and love through the trials? Will our marriage be a little taste of heaven? I'm glad I have Mark and Carol to show me how it's done.

Sinners Say "I Do" for the Time of Goodbye

Paul understood something important. While the inner renewal is the more important reality, there is no reversing or denying the reality of outer decay. Death is at work in each of us (2 Corinthians 4:12). The only question is when and how it will come.

Every marriage has its final moment. Usually death visits one spouse, grief the other. If the gospel has been treasured within the marriage, both spouses will be prepared. For the first one to go, a homecoming awaits him or her—the unimaginable experience of crossing between two worlds to arrive in the place for which we were created.

But in the mysterious providence of God, one spouse typically stays behind. The journey of one clay jar is not yet over. A trial of grief has begun, one that can shape each hour and exhaust every emotional fiber. Grief is a walk into the unknown, a universal experience played out in intensely personal ways. As C. S. Lewis reflected during his own grief over the loss of his wife, "No one ever told me that grief felt so like fear."[3] Yet, even in the darkest moments of loss, we long to please God in our grief. We don't grieve as those who have no hope (1 Thessalonians 4:13), because we do have hope—amazing, captivating, exultant hope. The resurrection of the Savior has guaranteed that. The fire of gospel hope burns deep, even when we feel incapable of feeding it.

A Story of Release and Hope: Jere and Albert

Jere leaned close to Albert's ear. She wanted to make sure her words were heard, that they reached him as he lay suspended between two worlds. He was only in his second week of hospice care, but things were deteriorating quickly. He was no longer awake and his body was shutting down. "Honey, run to Jesus. Don't worry about me, he'll take care of me too. But you go on."

Jere had been married to Albert for forty-two years. She had spent the last eleven of them caring for him in his battle with cancer. There was the radiation, the medication, the side effects, and the daily battle with fear. God spared Albert long enough to arrest him with the gospel and to create some treasured memories in marriage. But ultimately the cancer prevailed.

Jere understood the score. She had feared this moment, but had determined on her knees before God that she would seek to serve her husband in his dying just as she had in his living. After all, Albert was a man of love and duty. She knew he would fight death unless he was convinced she could survive without him. "I'll be fine honey. You can wait for me there." She held his hand, and then he was gone.

In the valley of the shadow of death, Jere did not cling to her husband like he was an idol as he departed. She just let go. It was nothing like resignation. There was no throwing up of arms and saying, "Well, God, I guess this is all your game so I have to agree to your terms." No, there was a resolute confidence that God knew best and could be trusted. There was courage to face the future beyond marriage. That's called faith. It's the kind that says, "The Lord gives, the Lord takes away. Blessed be the name of the Lord" (Job 1:21). A divine hope illuminated Jere's grief.

In his Word, God offers truth that is saturated with a hope essential to Jere or any Christian suffering loss. "For this slight momentary affliction is preparing for us an eternal weight of glory beyond all comparison" (2 Corinthians 4:17). These realities inspire hope when jars of clay become broken beyond repair. When sinners say goodbye, those who remain should keep in mind the weighty realities of hope.

My Loss is Slight

The Greek word for "slight" in 2 Corinthians 4:17 means light in weight, easy to bear, without much substance. It's the same word Jesus used in Matthew 11:30 when he said, "My burden is light." Paul is not portraying pain as irrelevant or insignificant. We have probably all been close enough to the bereavement process to know that the pain of losing a loved one is real.

Nor is Paul attempting to trivialize affliction. He wants to elevate our perspective *above* affliction. The loss *is* real, but the pain need not become a crushing burden. In fact, the word "slight" is intentionally set in contrast to the "weight of glory beyond all comparison" that awaits us in heaven. "When Paul says his afflictions are light," writes John Piper, "he does not mean easy or painless. He means that compared to what is coming they are as nothing. Compared to the weight of glory coming, they are like feathers on the scale."[4] In this life, the death of a spouse is a defining moment that will mark us until we also die. But compared to where we are headed, it is but a slight change of course in the ocean of eternity.

Jere's grief was completely real. She had the sleeplessness, the apathy and mental listlessness, even the inability to remember what Albert looked like—after forty-two years of marriage! But she also had hope. Her confidence in God helped her to lift her eyes beyond herself. Faith began to produce good works in her. At first they were small—the will to get up in the morning, the courage to leave her house. But as she sowed obedience, she began to reap vision. People around her were suffering and she was free to help. She could bear her grief and still serve others. Her pastor at the time said, "She grieved, but she also threw herself with eagerness into the local church. She met with me to evaluate how she could serve the church. She got a job, but intentionally designed her schedule around how she could serve God's people. Albert's death launched her in a new direction and there was kindled a growing desire not to miss out on anything!"

My Trial is Momentary

No trial seems momentary. There is a consuming quality that infects every trial. It just keeps going, or so it seems. But God invites us to rise from the table and come around to the other side. He wants us to look over our lives from a different vantage point.

Just as "slight" is set off in 2 Corinthians against *"weight of glory,"* "momentary" is set off against *"eternal weight of glory."* When measured by eternity, this mortal life is but a breath, a vapor, a suspended cloud that quickly dissipates in the slightest breeze. Whatever trial you are in, it will end, and one day you will see it for what it truly is: momentary and slight.

Grief often seems to stretch out before us like a road winding through a long, low valley. Self-pity and fear are always begging to come along for the ride. That's how it was for Jere at first. Her initial thoughts were, *What am I going to do? All I've known is being a caretaker for eleven years and a homemaker for the entire forty-two.* But for the Christian, there are things more powerful than grief. There is hope for the future. There is service in the present. Most importantly, there is the cross, both in the past and ever-present.

The cross became the organizing point for Jere's life and the interpretive lens of her experience. "My understanding of what was accomplished for me on the cross and the sacrifice of Christ has made all the difference. There is nothing more important to me than the cross. What God has given me through losing my husband is a greater understanding of who Christ is and what he did for me and a powerful sense of the Holy Spirit's work within me." Jere saw that God sent his Son as a suffering Savior to die in her place. That meant there was great joy in following him, even into suffering. The suffering of her loss would not last. It was momentary.

Rather than give in to despair, Jere made daily, sometimes hourly, decisions to embrace God's sovereign grace and look beyond herself. She has decided to make her post-marriage years ones of "undistracted devotion" to her Savior and his church. She jumped into the singles ministry (hanging out with twenty-somethings), reached out to the elderly, and traveled to conferences with no other intention but to serve. Jere isn't home watching the clock of her life wind down. And she certainly isn't consuming herself with the pleasant activities of the retirement years. For more than a decade now she has given herself away—the power of grace working eternity out in her life.

My Loss is Preparatory

It's hard to think of pain as preparation. Whether it's a toothache or the loss of a spouse, pain just seems so obviously a right-now kind of experience that the future rarely enters our thinking.

But God invites us to see the pain of loss as preparation for something incomprehensible. Our present loss doesn't simply open the door to glory, it produces glory. "This slight momentary affliction is *preparing for us* an eternal weight of glory" (2 Corinthians 4:17). What's more, this glory is "beyond all comparison." Think about those three words for a moment. Paul can't even summon an analogy or illustration to help us understand the glory that lies beyond our pain! He says it's unfathomable, inconceivable, unimaginable, *beyond all comparison.* That's what the spouse who remains can look forward to: Incomparable glory.

Albert's funeral was more than eleven years ago. Sometimes Jere still can't believe she's been a widow that long. Her house—with its thirty-two years of memories of three kids being raised, holidays together, neighborhood parties, the place where husband and wife whispered their last "I love you's"—was sold ten years ago. That was hard. Now she lives alone in a comfortable one-bedroom apartment. But she's rarely there. There's too much to do!

Jere loves to study. Even now, in her seventies, her enthusiasm for learning new things is infectious. She regularly studies God's Word and good books. This not only prepares her soul for her Savior, but it gives her more to offer others. One mother of three teens said, "Through Jere's example and honesty, she has encouraged me and exhorted me to greater love for my Savior and greater diligence with my family. Not only that, but I now have a vision for how God will meet me when I am older."

Jere sees something that so many widows and widowers miss. With no more duties to her husband and children, God has freed her to pour herself into others, and Scripture makes that claim upon her (Titus 2:3–5). She's got a great philosophy of life, "A wise person is always preparing for the next stage," she says. "Well, I'm in the deep winter of my life. I want to live preparing for what's after that. I want to spend my time and money in a way that recognizes eternity." She doesn't waste time guessing about the future. She just prepares for it.

I want to be like that when I grow up. And if I'm not, I'll be without excuse. You see, Jere is not just an incredible example to me. She's my mom. And I'm right here on the front row, watching her race and cheering her on toward the finish.

This Day for That Day

Matthew Henry once said, "It ought to be the business of every day to prepare for our last day."[5] This Puritan pastor was conscious of finishing the race, and a vital part of that race is the tandem relay that begins when sinners say "I do." At the beginning of this book I asked you to look hard at sin and how it plays out in the covenant of marriage, the most intimate and significant of human relationships. I hope you realize now that in looking at sin biblically we keep our eyes on what really matters in marriage: The unfathomable love and mercy of God poured out for us through the Savior.

When we gaze upon the cross, we begin to see the early light of a glorious day. Your marriage now, my marriage now, prepares us for that day. Marriage exists to point us and others to that day. What day is that? It's the Marriage Supper of the Lamb, what Charles Spurgeon describes as "the holiday of heaven." There's no better way to end this book than to stand beside Pastor Spurgeon and peek with him through the window of eternity, catching a small glimpse of what awaits us.

Heaven is always heaven, and unspeakably full of blessedness; but even heaven has its holidays, even bliss has its overflowings; [But] on that day when the springtide of the infinite ocean of joy shall have come, what a measureless flood of delight shall overflow the souls of all glorified spirits as they perceive that the consummation of love's great design is come—"The marriage of the Lamb is come, and his wife hath made herself ready"! We do not know yet, beloved, of what happiness we are capable . . . Oh, may I be there! . . . If I may but see the King in his beauty, in the fullness of his joy, when he shall take by the right hand her for whom he shed his precious blood, and shall know the joy which was set before him, for which he endured the cross, despising the shame, I shall be blest indeed! Oh, what a day that will be when every member of Christ shall be crowned in him, and with him, and every member of the mystical body shall be glorified in the glory of the Bridegroom! A day will come, the day of days, time's crown and glory, when . . . the saints, arrayed in the righteousness of Christ, shall be eternally one with him in living, loving, lasting union, partaking together of the same glory, the glory of the Most High. What must it be to be there![6]

Our marriages here are an imperfect picture of what we are looking forward to enjoying in eternal relationship with our Savior. I trust this book has given you a vision for how God is at work here for the sake of our joy there.

Friends, no matter where your marriage is at this time, it is pointing to the greatest reality possible. As real as our marriages are to us on this earth, they are just a shadow of the reality we will experience when Christ comes to claim his bride. Then we will have a wedding feast to celebrate our union with Christ that is unlike any feast that has ever been celebrated before. The entire family of Christ will be there—not one missing from the whole earth. The joy at that feast will not be marred by sin, struggle, pain, or disappointment. We will be forever with Christ in our new home. What glory is set before us as sinners who said, "I do."

Notes

Acknowledgments

1. John Piper, *A Godward Life* (Sisters, OR: Multnomah, 1997), 189.

Preface

1. Thomas Watson, *The Doctrine of Repentance* (Edinburgh: Banner of Truth Trust, repr. 1987), 63.
2. Horatio G. Spafford, "It Is Well With My Soul," verse 3, 1873.

Chapter 1

1. R. C. Sproul, *Knowing Scripture* (Downers Grove, IL: InterVarsity, 1978), 22.
2. George Knight, *Recovering Biblical Manhood and Womanhood: A Response to Evangelical Feminism*, ed. John Piper & Wayne Grudem (Wheaton, IL: Crossway, 1991), 175–176.
3. Cornelius Plantinga, *Not the Way It's Supposed to Be: A Breviary of Sin* (Grand Rapids, MI: Wm. B. Eerdmans, 1995), 199.
4. A.W. Tozer, *The Knowledge of the Holy* (San Francisco: HarperSanFrancisco, a division of HarperCollins Publishers, 1961), 1.

Chapter 2

1. Henry Scougal, *The Life of God in the Soul of Man: or The Nature and Excellency of the Christian Religion* (Harrisonburg, VA: Sprinkle Publications, 1986), 81.

2. Arnold A. Dallimore, *Spurgeon, A New Biography* (Edinburgh: Banner of Truth, 1987), 14.

3. John F. MacArthur, Jr., *The Vanishing Conscience: Drawing the Line in a No-Fault, Guilt-Free World* (Dallas: Word, 1994), 11.

4. Jerry Bridges, *The Discipline of Grace: God's Role and Our Role in the Pursuit of Holiness* (Colorado Springs: NavPress, 1994), 193.

5. J. I. Packer, *Rediscovering Holiness* (Ann Arbor: Servant Books, 1992), 135.

6. John Owen, *Sin and Temptation*, abridged and ed. by James M. Houston (Vancouver, B.C.: Regent, 1995), xvii.

Chapter 3

1. Doris Kearns Goodwin, *Team of Rivals* (New York: Simon and Schuster, 2005), 371.

2. And because all sin, whether in the confined battlefield of your heart or the larger battlefield of your marriage, is war against God, you are called in that regard simply to surrender to him: your goal is to confess, repent, and receive forgiveness.

3. John Newton, *Letters of John Newton*, no. 23 (Carlisle, PA: Banner of Truth Trust, reprinted 1990), 129.

4. Philip Yancey, *Soul Survivor* (New York: Doubleday, 2001), 58.

5. R. C. Sproul, *Pleasing God* (Wheaton, IL: Tyndale House Publishers, reissue edition, 1994), 150.

6. Thomas Watson, *Doctrine of Repentance* (Edinburgh, Banner of Truth, 1988), 110.

Chapter 4

1. Graeme Goldsworthy, *Gospel and Wisdom: Goldsworthy Trilogy*, (Carlisle, UK: Paternoster Press, 2000), 528.

2. J. I. Packer, *A Quest for Godliness: A Puritan Vision of the Christian Life* (Wheaton, IL: Crossway Books, 1990), 118.

3. Nanci Hellmich, "Couples Manage Conflicts Best with Empathy, Respect, Love," *USA Today*, September 26, 2005, reprinted in *The News Journal*, Wilmington, DE.

4. John Calvin, *Institutes*, ed. Battles, (Louisville-London: Westmnster John Knox Press, 1960), 604. John Calvin put it this way, "We teach that

all human desires are evil, and charge them with sin—not in that they are natural, but because they are inordinate."

Chapter 5

1. Kevin A. Miller, "Character," in *Christian Leadership: Cultivating a Leader's Heart,* ed. David Goetz (Wheaton, IL: Tyndale House Publishers, 2001), 26.

2. Jonathan Edwards, *Charity and Its Fruits* (reprint, Carlisle, PA: The Banner of Truth Trust, 1998), 157.

3. In their book *Relationships, A Mess Worth Making* (Cincinnati: New Growth Press, 2007), Tim Lane and Paul Tripp cover some of the themes of mercy applied to relationships in general.

4. Paul Tripp, *Instruments in the Redeemer's Hand* (Phillipsburg, N.J.: Presbyterian & Reformed, 2002), 136–137.

5. Susannah Wesley, born in 1669, was known as the "Mother of Methodism." She was a pastor's wife and the mother of nineteen children, nine of whom survived into adulthood. Throughout her life she experienced many hardships and griefs. Her sons Charles and John became two of the founders of Methodism, a revival that emphasized the methodical study of the Bible and holy living.

6. John Stott, *Basic Christian Leadership: Biblical Models of Church, Gospel and Ministry* (Downers Grove, IL: InterVarsity Press, 2002), 38.

7. William Shakespeare, *The Merchant of Venice,* 4.1.179–182, eds. Stephen Greenblatt et al. (New York, London: W.W. Norton, 1997).

Chapter 6

1. Available at http://en.wikipedia.org/wiki/31st_G8_summit.

2. A case can be made that we can forgive someone inaccessible to us because of death, distance, or denial. But this is a marriage book where sin plays out between two people who sleep in the same bed. So for our purposes we're going to look at the person-to-person relationship experience of forgiveness.

3. "Humiliation," from *The Valley of Vision: A Collection of Puritan Prayers and Devotions,* ed. Arthur S. Bennett (Edinburgh: Banner of Truth, 1975), 143.

4. R. T. France, *Tyndale New Testament Commentaries: Matthew* (Leicester, England: InterVarsity Press, 1985), 277.

5. Ken Sande, *The Peacemaker* (Grand Rapids, MI: Baker Books, 1991), 163.

6. John Newton, *Letters of John Newton*, no. 24 (Edinburgh: Banner of Truth, 1988), 132–133.

Chapter 7

1. Tom Carter, comp., *2200 Quotations from the Writings of Charles H. Spurgeon* (Grand Rapids, MI: Baker Books, 1988), 172.

2. Matthew Henry, *The Quietness and Meekness of Soul* (Morgan: PA: Soli Deo Gloria), 113.

3. J. I. Packer, *Knowing God* (Downer's Grove, Il.: InterVarsity Press, 1993), 90–91.

4. David Powlison, *Suffering and the Sovereignty of God* (Wheaton, Il.: Crossway Books, 2006), 145.

5. Dr. Martin Luther, *Works of Martin Luther*, trans. & eds. Adolph Spaeth, L. D. Reed, Henry Eyster Jacobs, et al. (Philadelphia: A. J. Holman Co., 1915), vol. 1, 29–38, Disputation of Dr. Martin Luther on the power and efficacy of indulgences, 1517.

6. A. W. Tozer, Chapter 9: "Meekness and Rest" in *The Pursuit of God*, (Camp Hill, PA: Christian Publications, Inc.).

7. C. J. Mahaney, *Humility, True Greatness* (Sisters, Oregon: Multnomah, 2005), 98.

Chapter 8

1. I recommend these books on romance: *Love That Lasts* by Gary and Betsy Ricucci; *Sex, Romance and the Glory of God* by C. J. Mahaney; *Sex and the Supremacy of Christ* by John Piper; and *The Intimate Marriage* by R. C. Sproul.

2. J. I. Packer, *God's Words* (Downer's Grove, IL: InterVarsity Press, 1981), 95–96.

3. Cornelius Plantinga, *Not the Way It's Supposed To Be: A Breviary of Sin* (Grand Rapids, MI: Wm. B. Eerdmans Pub. Co., 1995), 199.

4. John Stott, *The Message of 1 Timothy and Titus* (Leicester, England; Inter-Varsity Press, 1996) 193.

5. Andrew A. Bonar, *Life and Remains: Letters, Lectures and Poems of the Rev. Robert Murray M'Cheyne, Minister of St. Peter's Church, Dundee* (New York: Robert Carter, 1848), 209.

6. Jerry Bridges, *Disciplines of Grace* (Colorado Springs: NavPress, 1994), 21.

7. John Owen, *Sin and Temptation* (Portland: Multnomah, 1983, repr. Vancouver, B.C.: Regent College, 1995), 36–37.

Chapter 9

1. From *Dictionary of Paul and His Letters*, 172–173, "As a wealthy hub for commerce and seafarers, Greek Corinth was evidently renowned for its vice, especially its sexual corruption, and for its many religious temples and rites. Aristophanes (c. 450–385 B.C.) even coined the term *korinthiazesthai* ("to act like a Corinthian," i.e. "to commit fornication") in view of the city's reputation. Plato used the term "Corinthian girl" as a euphemism for a prostitute. And although its historical accuracy is disputed, Strabo's account of 1000 prostitutes in the temple of Aphrodite does reflect the city's image, in which the many temples played their own role in the immoral tenor of its life."

2. John F. MacArthur, *1 Corinthians Commentary* (Chicago: Moody Publishers, 1984), ix.

3. R. C. Sproul, *The Intimate Marriage* (Phillipsburg, NJ: P & R Publishing, 1975, reissue 2003), 89.

4. Sixty percent of all website visits are sexual in nature (*MSNBC Survey 2000)*; Hollywood currently releases 11,000 adult movies per year – more than twenty times the mainstream movie production (*LA Times Magazine, 2002); One in four American adults surveyed in 2002 admitted to seeing an x-rated movie in the last year. (*National Opinion Research Letter); http://www.blazinggrace.org/pornstatistics.htm).

5. One of the great challenges in embracing a biblical view of sex in marriage is that our present experience can be so discouraging and seem so hopeless. We may bring great guilt or shame into our marriage from things we've done or things that have been done to us in life. And our sexual interactions in marriage may have been unloving, manipulative, or lust-driven. These struggles are real and powerful. My hope is that in reading this chapter you will begin to catch a vision for what sex CAN be, and begin to work together to make that more and more your experience. If there is one thing I know, it is that the gospel's transforming power can reach into any relationship or experience and bring life and joy where there has been defeat and regret.

6. John Piper, *Desiring God* (Sisters, OR: Multnomah, 1996), 175.

7. C. J. Mahaney, *Sex, Romance and the Glory of God: What Every Christian Husband Needs to Know* (Wheaton, IL: Crossway Books, 2004), 79.

8. Gary and Betsy Ricucci, *Love That Lasts: When Marriage Meets Grace* (Wheaton, IL: Good News-Crossway Books, 2006), 117.

Chapter 10

1. J. I. Packer, *A Quest for Godliness* (Wheaton, IL: Crossway Books, 1990, repr. Richard Baxter, *Works* IV: 234, *The Poor Man's Family Book*, 1674).

2. D. A. Carson, *How Long, O Lord?* (Grand Rapids, MI: Baker Books, 1990), 109.

3. C. S. Lewis, *A Grief Observed* (New York: Harper Collins, 1961), 3.

4. John Piper (sermon, Bethlehem Baptist Church, Minneapolis, MN, September 6, 1992).

5. Quoted by Randy Alcorn, *In Light of Eternity* (Colorado Springs, CO: Waterbrook Press, 1999), 137.

6. C. H. Spurgeon, The Marriage of the Lamb, no. 2096 (sermon, Metropolitan Tabernacle, Newington, England, Lord's Day morning, July 21, 1889).

Dave Harvey is the Pastor of Preaching at *Four Oaks Community Church* in Tallahassee, Florida. Dave has 27 years of pastoral experience and has traveled nationally and internationally teaching Christians, equipping pastors and training church planters. He served on the Sovereign Grace Ministries Leadership Team for 17 years and continues to serve on the board of the *Christian Counseling and Educational Foundation (CCEF)*. Dave has a DMin from Westminster Theological Seminary, is the author of *Am I Called?*, *Rescuing Ambition, When Sinners Say "I Do"*, and is a contributing author to *Worldliness: Resisting the Seduction of a Fallen World.*

Resources for *When Sinners Say "I Do"*

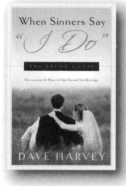

Study Guide

For each chapter of book:
Gospel Implications
Gospel Applications
   For Me
   For Us
Gospel Interaction
   for Small Group Discussion

ISBN: 978-0-9815400-1-6
www.shepherdpress.com

Book available in Spanish
ISBN: 978-0-9824387-1-8

Audio Book

Read by the author

ISBN: 978-09767582-9-7
www.shepherdpress.com